Without Parachutes

How I Survived 1,000 Attack Helicopter Combat Missions in Vietnam

One Soldier's story about how attack helicopter operating rules developed during the early days of the Vietnam War helped him survive three years of combat.

Jerry W. Childers
Colonel, US Army (Retired)

authorHOUSE™
1663 Liberty Drive, Suite 200
Bloomington, Indiana 47403
(800) 839-8640
www.AuthorHouse.com

First published by AuthorHouse 12/02/05

ISBN: 1-4208-8258-9 (sc)
ISBN: 1-4208-8259-7 (dj)

Library of Congress Control Number: 2005908168

Printed in the United States of America
Bloomington, Indiana

This book is printed on acid-free paper.

APPRECIATION

For my wife Mary Jane, and our children, William, Thomas and in memory of Nonna, who shared the pains of frequent and extended family separations, dozens of household movements and constant life-style disruptions in order that I might have the freedom to pursue my dreams.

CONTENTS

INTRODUCTION

My grandfather John Miller served in the U.S. Army for about ten years. All I know about his service is that he was a sniper in the U.S. Infantry, and that he fired the first shots of some important battle during the Moro rebellion in the Philippines. I would like to know more, much more. Unfortunately, he left no records and his story is lost.

I recently looked back on my own thirty three years of military training and active service. Unlike my grandfather, I decided to record my story. I served three combat tours in Vietnam and was directly involved in helping move U.S. Army Aviation from a small post-Korean War medical evacuation and reconnaissance force to a full combat arms branch as seen in Iraq.

My military training started in 1957, and I retired in 1990, fifteen years before this was written. Many names, dates and places have long since slipped my mind. However, through research on the Internet and use of my dusty files, I have surprised even myself on the amount of detail I have been able to recover.

I also discussed some of my memories with other retired soldiers who participated in the events. As might be expected, the view from their cockpit sometimes differed from mine. I apologize in advance for any inaccuracies that might be contained herein.

Some might ask why I did not write this story earlier when my memory was fresher. As you read this you will see that many events relate to painful experiences that involve the death of friends and subordinates. Such is the nature of a military career, especially one that focused on aviation and combat, as was mine.

Over the years I was successful in keeping these stories pushed into the back of my mind. As they recently came forward and were recorded, some of the pain returned. I have attempted to keep emotion and bloody details out, but in some cases, the need to be accurate ruled. Some stories may not be suitable for younger readers.

The military is notorious for its use of acronyms in dialog. These abbreviations serve as a sort of shorthand that expedites complex discussions among those on the inside. Since military acronyms tend to bewilder those without a related background, I have made every effort to minimize their use. Where they are used, I have provided the full terminology along with the acronym the first time it appears.

IN MEMORIAM

In November 1964, I arrived in Vietnam as part of a group of about forty replacement pilots. The next day we were called to a meeting to receive unit assignments. Prior to issuing the orders, the personnel officer offered us the opportunity to volunteer for the Utility Tactical Transport Helicopter Company (UTT) in Saigon. He told us that the UTT was the only armed helicopter company in Vietnam, and that because of the special nature of its mission and its high casualty rate, all of its aircrew members were volunteers. He then asked if anyone would like to volunteer. Four of us raised our hands. I am the only one of those four to have survived that year. I dedicate this book to the memory of those three who died in 1965, and fifteen others that died while serving under my command during a later tour in 1972-73. The stories surrounding their loss are told in this book.

1965

CPT LYAL HANCIL ERWIN
CW2 BILLY GENE HAMMER
1LT CARL JOSEPH MANGOLD

1972-73

CPT STEVEN DALE HOWARD
CW2 JAMES MITCHELL STEVER
CW2 RONALD LEE VANLANDINGHAM
WO1 ANTHONY DAL POZZO, JR

SP5 JAMES LELAND SCROGGINS
SP5 DAVID EDWARDS WISCHEMANN
SP4 RAYMOND LEE GOODCHILD
SP4 JAMES DAVID BROWN
SP4 RICHARD BARTON FREEMAN
SP4 LOUIS OSCAR CALDERON
SP4 ROGER RIDGELY CHAMBLISS
SP4 MILTON CHARLES HUNTER
SP4 CHARLES LEROY STEWART, JR
SP4 DELBERT ROY WOOD
SP4 TIMOTHY ARMA THOMAS

Names, ranks and spelling as listed on the Vietnam Veterans Memorial Wall Web Site.

PROLOGUE

THE REVELATION

Our flight of UH-1 Huey helicopters was clawing its way through a bright blue sky one thousand feet above an intense green world of rice paddies and canals. The four other helicopters were locked in formation closely around me, our rotor blades overlapping. We were heavily loaded with infantry troops, getting ready to insert them on a combat assault in central Vietnam. We decreased power and started our descent toward the landing zone. Suddenly our world erupted in gunfire, some rounds going down but most coming up at us. The enemy had opened fire with automatic weapons and my door gunners were shooting back with their machine guns. Hot spent brass from the machine gun behind me rained on my helmet, some burning its way down the back of my shirt. The radios blasted calls of "receiving fire", "mayday" and "going down" in my earphones.

There was little time to worry about the bullets that were popping and hissing around me. I had to keep total focus on maintaining my position in the formation. One miscue and my rotor blades would strike those of another helicopter, immediately turning both aircraft into free falling boxes of death. Nobody would survive because unlike fixed wing combat crews, helicopter combat crews flew without parachutes.

Rounds were now striking my aircraft. A window shattered and a door gunner yelled "I'm hit". Small whisks of smoke started coming out of the helicopter in front of me. Then, without further warning, it burst into flames. At first slowly, then with increasing speed, the stricken helicopter scribed an arch of black smoke, finally crashing in a ball of fire. Now I was in the lead. The other aircraft in the flight were flying formation on me and the decisions I had to make in the next few seconds could mean life or death, not only to our aircrews but also for the dozens of infantry soldiers in our care.

Should I abort the approach? turn left? turn right? climb? descend? I pleaded for divine guidance. Suddenly, I heard a small voice inside my head say "go with the wind – go with the wind". What in the world did that mean? As I looked around seeking another clue, I noticed the death plume of greasy smoke from a crashed and burning aircraft. The smoke was blowing across my flight path from the right to the left at a good clip. Now I had it! I turned the flight left ninety degrees. By doing so, the wind was now pushing us about twenty miles per hour faster over the ground. The enemy bullets were no longer hitting in the cockpit, but were harmlessly hitting around the tail of the aircraft. The Vietcong gunners were still aiming one helicopter length in front of our aircraft as they had been taught. But since we were flying faster, their lead was not enough. In moments we were out of danger and on our way to the alternate landing zone.

I woke up with a start. It had all been a dream, but a special dream that would save my life several times over the next few years. I did not know it then, but I was destined to spend three years of my life flying helicopters in combat in Vietnam.

At the time of the dream I was a brand new Army Aviator assigned to the 11th Air Assault Division at Fort Benning, Georgia. The Division was soon going to be renamed the 1st Air Cavalry Division and deployed to Vietnam. It was September 1964, and my assault helicopter company was intensely training for deployment. Each day we were practicing tighter and tighter formation flying.

During a recent classroom training session older pilots who had already survived a tour in Vietnam told us war stories. Their vivid description of actual combat, and our daily formation flight training missions formed the genesis of my dream.

The dream took place three years into a twenty nine year active duty Army career. In order to place it in proper perspective, it is necessary to start at the beginning.

CHAPTER 1

THE EARLY YEARS

When I completed high school in 1957, I was in love with all things military. My father and all five of my parent's brothers had served in World War Two. I was there when they came home triumphantly in 1945. Later, I was old enough to follow the Korean War in the newspaper. I spent almost every Saturday after the age of seven at the local theater watching movies about war and cowboys. The good guys always won, and my view of the invincibility of the American fighting man was colored by this propaganda. My rude awakening to the horrors of war would not come until 1964, when I first experienced combat. Therefore, upon entering college I was pleased to find myself enrolled in the Army Reserve Officer Training Corps (ROTC). In those days all healthy males who entered a state land grant college were required to take two years of ROTC. The second two years were voluntary and could lead to a commission as an officer, and active duty.

During my first two years at Tennessee Tech at Cookeville, Tennessee, I joined the ROTC precision drill team. We trained for long hours and traveled throughout the region to participate in drill competitions. This activity became the focus of my attention and my grades suffered as a result. During my second year I was promoted to Cadet Sergeant and given the job as one of three squad leaders on the team. At the end of that year I was admitted to the advanced ROTC course, but was not successful in my quest to command the drill team.

Only one junior could serve on the team. He held the rank of Cadet Lieutenant and was the platoon leader. I badly wanted the job but somebody beat me out. I had learned a valuable life lesson about winning and losing. Wanting something was not enough. You had to go get it or somebody else would. As a consolation, I was appointed a Company First Sergeant in one of the line companies for my third year.

Between my third and fourth year I attended eight weeks of ROTC summer camp at Fort Benning, Georgia. There were probably twelve hundred cadets from all over the South at that camp. It was essentially basic combat training with a focus on leadership. We were assigned leadership positions that changed on a daily basis, and were closely graded on our performance.

During the course we were administered a leadership reaction test. We were rotated through a series of about twelve stations and were presented with a difficult simulated combat leadership problem at each one of them. To my surprise, I was graded at near the top of all cadets in leadership potential during that summer camp.

Upon return to school, I was promoted to Cadet Captain and served as a company commander throughout my senior year. More importantly, I was designated a distinguished military student, and upon graduation, was offered a commission in the regular Army. The offered commission was to be in the Quartermaster Corps. However, before reporting for quartermaster duty, I would have to attend airborne and ranger training, then spend two years in an infantry assignment.

I was also offered a reserve commission in the Artillery Branch. This assignment would have required some initial training at Fort Bliss, Texas, with a subsequent assignment to Germany. The reserve commission would lead to a part time job and a civilian career. The regular commission would lead to a military career, and was the same commission awarded to West Point graduates. I had to decide between the two.

To the dismay of my ROTC Instructors, I elected to turn down the much sought after regular commission and enter the reserves. This decision was reached because I was engaged to get married a week after graduation, and the artillery assignment at Fort Bliss, Texas offered more stability. If I had taken the regular commission, it would have been many months before I reported to a stable duty station. This would have meant months of separation from my new bride.

I also did not like the idea of the Quartermaster Corps. My father-in-law, who had been a First Sergeant in the horse cavalry and served in the Quartermaster Corps at the beginning of World War Two, jokingly told me that as a quartermaster officer, I would be "counting socks in a warehouse somewhere up north." Thus, the choice was easy and was in retrospect, one of the best and most important career decisions I would make. After my first tour in Vietnam I would be offered a regular commission again, this time in the artillery, which was the branch I wanted. I took the offer.

Shortly before graduation, I had my first opportunity to see and touch a helicopter. My ROTC class went on a field trip to Fort Campbell, Kentucky to get a look at the 'real' Army. I was highly impressed by their Commander, Major General William Westmoreland, who personally welcomed us to the 101st Airborne 'Screaming Eagle' Division for the day. Little did I know that he would soon be my commander in Vietnam, and that in about twenty five years I would serve as the Chief of Staff of the Division and Fort Campbell.

Sometime during our visit with the Screaming Eagles, we toured a display of Army equipment. Included was a small bubble helicopter known as the Bell OH-13 Sioux (all Army helicopters, except the AH-1 Cobra, are named after American Indian tribes). The Sioux is the aircraft you see carrying wounded soldiers in the MASH television series.

I don't recall being very impressed with the machine or the pilot. I did, however, notice his sunglasses, flight suit and helmet. If someone had told me at that time that within five years, I would be serving as an Army helicopter test pilot at the Bell Helicopter assembly plant near Fort Worth, Texas, I would have laughed in their face.

My bride to be, Mary Jane, had graduated from college in the summer of 1961 and obtained a job as a juvenile probation officer with the State of Tennessee. She was not yet twenty one years old, and herself a juvenile. She lived and worked in Murfreesboro, Tennessee while I completed my last semester of college. I graduated in mid-December 1961, and we were married one week later. To her horror she had been unable to get a marriage license until her parents signed the application because she was under-age.

We lived in an apartment in Murfreesboro for one month and departed on 27 January 1962 for Fort Bliss, near El Paso Texas. That became the date of my official entry onto active duty in the Army. We loaded everything we owned into the back of a 1956 Chevrolet station wagon. It was not our first car. Mary Jane's father had helped her buy a 1961 Ford Falcon when she went to work. It was a very small car and I was a Chevrolet man. I traded it off within two weeks of getting married. Of course, I inherited the car note which amounted to about eighteen hundred dollars. Over the years I have enjoyed telling friends that we started our married life with a net worth of less than zero.

The trip to Texas took two days and would have been uneventful if the Chevrolet had been equipped with an operational fuel gage. I had to guess how far we could go without refueling. I got it wrong somewhere south of Dallas when the tank went dry as I tried to make it to one more town. The engine died near a crossroads with an underpass, so I walked down and around to look for a gas station. What I found was a man and woman in an old coupe being very friendly with each other. After we all recovered, they took me a few miles to get a can of gas.

Freshly refueled, we proceeded on our way and at dark we were still a long way from El Paso. We were determined to make it in that night so I continued to drive. At about 10:00 PM we spotted the city lights and thought we were there. However, it took us another two hours driving at seventy five mph to get there. We were astonished at the clear air and great visibility of southwest Texas. The next morning I reported to the appointed place and started my military career.

Upon arrival at Fort Bliss I entered the Air Defense Artillery Basic Officer's Course. The course lasted about eight weeks while we studied the organization and equipment of the Army's air defense forces. Our focus was on the Army's Nike Hercules medium range air defense rocket. It was a two stage radar directed rocket with a range of about one hundred miles. This system was at that time deployed at fixed locations in Europe, Korea and the United States. About half of the sixty men in my class went to Nike units following graduation.

I was ordered to join a new Hawk missile battalion being formed there at Fort Bliss for deployment to Europe. The Hawk was a single stage mobile missile with a range of several miles. It had been designed to travel with the Army in the field. Before reporting, I attended a three week long course to get qualified on the Hawk. At about that time Mary Jane started suffering with morning sickness, so we knew our life was about to take a drastic turn.

While in school I enjoyed several food firsts. Being from the mountains of North Carolina and Tennessee, I had been raised on fried chicken, pork and beef. At the Fort Bliss officers club I got my first taste of grilled beef and lobster. The beef was great but I never acquired a taste for lobster or any other kind of seafood. However, I grew to love Mexican food and some of the liquid refreshments from across the border at Juarez.

I joined C Battery of the 8th Battalion, 7th Artillery on 28 March 1962. It was the second Hawk battalion in a series that was being formed to field the new missile system. The first one had recently deployed to Fort Meade, Maryland. I was assigned as was the platoon leader of the Fire Control and Launcher Platoon. I had two Second Lieutenants who worked for me. One was responsible for the fire control section and the other responsible for the launcher section of the platoon.

Both of my Lieutenants attended the same courses I had just completed, and reported to the unit on the same day I reported. However, since their hometowns were closer to Fort Bliss than mine, they had been given only one day of travel time instead of the two days I received. Because our active duty entry date was determined by the day we started travel, I had one day of rank on them and thus was their boss for the next year and a half. This was my first introduction to the unbendable date of rank system in the Army.

We trained for several months in classrooms and in the desert surrounding Fort Bliss. The first subject I was assigned to teach was on the fifty caliber machine gun. I was to teach a group of about eighty men how to set the 'head space and timing' on the gun. I had never touched a fifty caliber, so had to pull out a book and quickly read it before I could teach the class. Most of our Sergeants were better qualified to teach the class than I was. They had served in the Korean War and some had used the weapon in combat. Needless to say, I did not approach the class with a lot of confidence. However, I must have done a pretty good job because I was selected to present it to the other three batteries in the battalion.

I proudly display missiles and a launcher at a parade in Maryland in 1963

I was later ordered to plan and conduct a field training exercise involving the battery in its initial occupation of a new field position. On a whim, I bought some firecrackers to spice up simulated enemy activity. It was such a hit with the chain of command that I ended up conducting it for the other batteries. The firecrackers got expensive but the effort paid off later when I had to struggle to get my flight school application approved.

As the battery completed training we conducted a graduation exercise during which I was allowed to track a target drone and fire a live Hawk missile at it. I can still feel the big boom as the missile left the launcher. It was the biggest thing to date in my military life but the excitement was somewhat dampened when the missile failed to destroy the target. The miss was not my fault. The proximity fuse had been defective.

I had completed training and was preparing for deployment to Germany when several events occurred that would forever change the course of my life. The battery was called in one night and briefed on the Cuban Missile Crisis, which was just starting. We drew live missiles and moved into the desert near the runways at Biggs Air Force

Base, adjacent to Fort Bliss. Our mission was to protect the nuclear equipped B-52 bombers that flew out of the Base. I will never forget seeing those heavily loaded bombers taking off, pouring black exhaust trails out of their eight engines, carrying their nuclear bombs. I had seen hundreds of them take off before but nothing like that. It seemed to take forever for them to gain enough speed to climb above a few feet off of the ground.

On the second morning of the Crisis, I was told to grab a Jeep and go to the Army hospital. My son Bill had been born. Left alone, Mary Jane had asked a neighbor to drive her to the hospital. Nevertheless, it was a happy event. I remember both pride and fear. I was extremely proud of my healthy new son and his healthy mother. But President Kennedy was making frequent speeches to the Nation on television and radio, and there was much uncertainty in the air. Fortunately, Mary Jane was somewhat insulated from it all. In those days the new mothers spent several days in the Hospital so the crisis was essentially over by the time she went home.

At the end of the third day we were told to re-deploy out of the field location and begin loading our equipment on railroad cars for movement to Florida. Before we were ready to go, there was a train derailment near Waco that closed the tracks for about three days. The Army decided we could not get to Florida soon enough so they told us to stay put. They deployed the Hawk Battalion from Fort Meade, Maryland to take our place. We were ordered to move to Maryland to replace them.

In thirty six hours I had gone from Germany bound to Florida bound to Maryland bound. The battalion that went to Florida stayed there for years. I have often wondered how my life would have been different if that train had not wrecked. The Army was certainly turning out to be an interesting place to work, and I was getting hooked.

Our movement to Fort Meade proceeded a few weeks later. Mary Jane and the baby flew to Tennessee and I drove the car by myself. The Chevrolet's voltage regulator went out on the second day of the trip and by the time I got to Tennessee, all of the wiring had burned out. It took several days and about two hundred dollars, or about a month's pay, to get it fixed.

Upon arrival at Fort Meade we were assigned family quarters. Our apartment was on the third floor and the laundry room was in the basement. Mary Jane was not pleased to say the least. Neither was she pleased with our old Chevrolet. We could afford only a few dollars worth of gas at a time so I would get about one call a month that she was stranded somewhere out of gas. I never did get that gas gage fixed.

The battalion spent a lot of time in the field so Mary Jane was often left to take care of our home and our new child. This was to become the story of our years in the military. Some time in the Summer of 1963, I deployed on a huge training exercise called Swift Strike Three. It took place throughout the Southeastern United States and involved all Services. Our Battalion traveled by road convoy to South Carolina where we deployed and played war games for weeks.

At one point we set-up our battery in a large watermelon patch. It had already been picked but there were lots of small melons still on the ground. All of us enjoyed our fill of this wonderful fruit. However, one of my soldiers, a truck mechanic named Private First Class Mapes, stuffed himself with watermelon, and then decided to take a dip in a farm pond. He somehow got choked on the melon and drowned. I helped pull him out of the water and had my first sad experience of dealing with death and the writing of a letter of condolence to the next of kin. Unfortunately, I was to write them many times in the years to come.

Near the end of the exercise I was ordered to make a reconnaissance of a potential new place to locate the battery. Since it was some distance away, I was allocated a helicopter to do the job. At the appointed time the aircraft arrived. It was an old cargo helicopter called a CH-19 Chickasaw. This aircraft is what we now call a first generation helicopter, and had seen its first use during the Korean War. As far as I was concerned, it was a Cadillac. There was only a Warrant Officer pilot on board, so he allowed me to sit in the copilot's seat throughout the flight. We probably spent no more than an hour in the air but it was enough to convince me that flying was for me.

A few days later on a cool, rainy morning, a small helicopter delivered a one star Army General to our battery area for a visit. This was the first real General I remember seeing. The pilot, a Warrant Officer, landed the aircraft on a mud flat. The General exited the aircraft and stepped in mud up to his ankles. He waded off with our commander to tour the area. I looked back and the pilot had his feet propped up on the instrument panel. He was pouring himself a cup of coffee from a thermos jug. I looked at him and I looked at the General slopping through the mud and right then and there, I knew which one I wanted to emulate. Little did I know that deciding to become a pilot was essentially the kiss of death if you aspired to be an Army General. I would find this out the hard way later in life.

CHAPTER 2

IN PURSUIT OF WINGS

Immediately upon return from Swift Strike Three I started the flight school application process. The key requirements were to successfully pass an aptitude test, pass a flight physical and get approval of your chain of command. I visited the library and checked out every book they had on learning to fly. After weeks of careful study I was well prepared for the aptitude test. When I took it, I passed with flying colors.

The flight physical was another matter. I passed everything but the eye test the first time around. My far vision was 20/25, while the requirement to start flight school was 20/20. As I understood it, this meant that I had to get within twenty feet of a wall chart to read it when the qualified applicant could read from twenty five feet. I decided to rest my eyes as much as possible for a few weeks then retake the physical. I completely stopped reading and looking at television. I would come home from work and lay with a towel over my eyes until bedtime. I also exercised my eyes frequently. Something worked because on the retake my eyes were rated at 20/15. It was a happy day when I found out that I was physically qualified for flight school.

With a completed application in hand I approached my battery commander. He reluctantly added his recommendation for approval and forwarded it the battalion commander, who had to recommend either approval or disapproval. If he approved, it would be forward to the Pentagon for a decision. His first reaction was to disapprove it. I requested permission to talk to him and informed him that I was a reserve officer who was scheduled for release from active duty in about four months. I also told him that if I could go to flight school, I would stay in the Army. After considering these facts he reluctantly decided to approve my application. He told me aviation was a dead end street and that I would never again be promoted. Little did we know that I was to be promoted early (known as being in the top 5 percent) three times and would be a selected for promotion to full colonel with only eighteen years of service.

The flight school application was forwarded to The Department of the Army in Washington, D.C. About two weeks after it left Fort Meade, I called to see if it had been received. They had it and said that it would be months before I could be programmed into a class. They asked me if I could move on short notice if someone who was already scheduled dropped out. I told them I could leave with a few days notice. Sure enough, I was notified a couple of weeks later that I was to report to Fort Wolters, Texas for primary helicopter flight training in about seven days.

Most of the furniture in our quarters belonged to the Army so it was easy to pack and get on the road with such short notice. We were somewhat slowed because Mary Jane was again experiencing morning sickness. I dropped her and Bill in Tennessee and traveled on alone to Fort Wolters. Upon reporting for duty I was issued my flight gear. When they handed me that flight helmet and sunglasses, I knew I had really arrived and was not dreaming. We were assigned family housing on post. As soon as our household goods arrived, Mary Jane and family drove down to join me.

At that time the demand for Army Aviators in Vietnam was small. Therefore, the Army planned for at least one third of each class to wash out (fail the course) during the first few weeks of training. They assigned each instructor three students to start with and obviously he was motivated to get rid of one of them as quickly as possible to lower his workload. They would wash a student out for the slightest reason and there was no appeal. Some students just didn't have the coordination or aptitude to fly a helicopter. Others were not willing to work with sufficient energy. Some failed the academic course. Before long, almost half of our class was gone.

We routinely went to class in the mornings and flew in the afternoons. In the classroom we studied all of the aircraft systems with special attention to procedures to be followed if an emergency occurred. We also studied navigation, map reading, weather, airframe maintenance and a lot of other subjects. I had no problems mastering the subject material.

The afternoons were the best part of the day. After weather and safety briefings the instructor would fly with one student to an outlying airfield while the rest of the class rode a bus. These fields were called stage fields. They consisted of four or five short runways set side by side so several aircraft could train at the same time. We would each get about an hour of flying time, then a different student would fly back to the base with the instructor.

I recall the first time I climbed into our training aircraft. It was an OH-23 Raven with three side-by-side seats, and was by far the hardest aircraft to fly the Army ever owned. The rotor system was equipped with a set of paddles to control its tilt, which determined the direction in which the aircraft flew: forward, backward or sideways. These paddles were controlled by the cyclic stick, which was held in our right hand. In our left hand we held the collective stick which controlled the pitch or 'bite' of the blades. It moved up or down to make the machine move up or down. On the end of the collective, and also held in the pilots left hand was a motorcycle type twist grip that was the throttle. We used the throttle to control engine revolutions per minute (RPM). The RPM had to be held constant at all times so the pilot had to simultaneously watch the engine gages and roll throttle on or off as needed.

OH-23 Raven we used for flight training in 1963 at Fort Wolters. One of 2 paddles that controlled the rotor blades is visible at upper left.

The final set of controls was the pedals. You pushed with a foot on one or the other of them to cause the aircraft to rotate about its center line when at a hover, and to keep the aircraft coordinated (not flying sideways) when in forward flight. To properly fly the aircraft all of the controls were in constant motion. Any change in one would generate a need to change the others, which generated more needs. Then the changing air currents caused by the wind and other aircraft flying nearby caused more changes. To this day I cannot understand how a human could fly one of those old helicopters.

It took me about eight flying hours to master hovering, taking off, landing, and emergency landings called auto-rotations. Throughout the first few hours of flying the instructor would suddenly turn off the engine and see if I could make an emergency landing. This required an instantaneous lowering of the collective to maintain RPM, and turning the aircraft into the wind toward a clearing in the trees. We had to mentally calculate the glide angle (which was almost straight down in the OH-23) and be able to fly the aircraft into the selected clearing, slow the aircraft down by raising the nose, then pull the collective up just enough to soften our landing. Throughout all my years of flying the auto-rotation was easily the most critical of all maneuvers performed in a helicopter. I got pretty good at it and my proficiency was to save me, my aircraft and my crew several times over the years.

When the instructor thought a student was ready to solo, he would step out of the aircraft and let him go for his first flight alone. During the flight you had to make three successful takeoffs, trips around the airfield, and landings. This moment lives as clearly in my mind as the firing of the Hawk missile. I was so busy doing everything I had been taught that I did not notice I was alone in the aircraft until flying at one thousand feet downwind to prepare for landing. Suddenly I noticed the instructor's cyclic moving in front of his now empty seat. For the first time I had a clear view of it since he was now gone. It took me a few seconds to realize that I moving the controls. If someone was watching closely from the ground, I am sure they saw the aircraft lurch a bit as I regained my composure.

After the first solo it was customary for other pilots to rip off your shirt when you exited your aircraft. Since we wore flight suits, we were allowed to pull them off so our tee shirt could be torn away. Then everybody took a felt tip pen and autographed what was left of the shirt. It was a happy event and was executed with enthusiasm. Many pilots saved their torn shirts for souvenirs. Like so many other items, mine became lost in the years of moving about in the Army.

Several events occurred during this phase of flight training that is worth recalling. The first of these was the death of President Kennedy. We were in an afternoon briefing session when the chief instructor came in and gave us the news. The room was quiet for several minutes as the disbelief sunk in. We were released for the rest of the day to go home and follow events on television. The next day we attended a memorial service then went on with business as usual.

About halfway through the training two student pilots and two instructors were killed when they collided in mid-air. One aircraft had somehow flown up underneath the other with predictable results. For days we all made an extra effort to watch out for other aircraft. The mid-air collision became our worst fear during peacetime flying. Later in my flying career, when the Army introduced nap-of-the-earth flying and night vision goggle operations, wire strikes would become our worst fear. I can recall literally dozens of fatal accidents caused by mid-air collisions and wire strikes.

A third significant event at Fort Wolters was the birth of our Daughter Nonna. Again, Mary Jane had to get herself to the hospital. This time I was taking a check ride with an instructor. These rides were scheduled as various points during the training to judge our progress. If we passed, we got a white grade slip. If we failed, we got a pink grade slip. A pink slip usually meant you had washed out of flight school.

On this day, I got a daughter and also got a pink slip. Here I was once more, happy and sad at the same time. After a joyous visit with my healthy daughter and her healthy mother, I returned to the flight line and explained the situation to my instructor. He knew I had been nervous during the check ride and convinced the chief instructor to let me take the ride over again. This time I was successful and we were on our way to Fort Rucker, Alabama for advanced flight training.

As I drove in the gate of the Army Aviation Center at Fort Rucker in my old Chevy station wagon, the first thing saw was a UH-1 Huey helicopter hovering beside the road. The UH-1 was officially given the Indian tribe name 'Iroquois' but became fondly known as the Huey.

My heart leapt as I realized how big it was and that I would soon be flying it.

We could not get a house on base so we rented a small one outside the gate in the town of Ozark. After getting the family settled, I reported in to find out that I was scheduled to learn to fly the CH-34 Choctaw cargo helicopter during the first phase of my advanced training. I also found out that my stick partner (other student that flew with the same instructor), was to again be a Vietnamese Air Force pilot named Cadet Nguyen Quy An. I had flown with him at Fort Wolters.

Flight school stick buddies at Fort Wolters. From left students Lieutenant George Fourson, me, instructor, and Cadet An of the Vietnamese Air Force

The CH-34 was a huge aircraft powered by the same engine that was then in use on passenger airliners. Half of our class flew these and half the CH-19 Chickasaw, which was the type in which I made the reconnaissance flight back in South Carolina. The CH-19 was old and no longer in operational use in our Army. However, the CH-34 was still in use and I was to get the chance to see it in action in Vietnam, and fly it during a later assignment. All Vietnamese students flew the CH-34 because it was the type with which their Air Force was equipped. I was selected to continue as Cadet An's stick buddy, so joined him in learning to fly the CH-34.

The CH-34 had a reputation as being a 'Widow Maker.' It was constructed mostly of magnesium and aluminum, and used a highly volatile aviation gasoline with an octane rating about fifty percent higher that automobile fuel. The aircraft would immediately burn to a crisp if it crashed. This occurred at Fort Benning, Georgia during our training when one tried to make an emergency landing in the center of a divided highway. The wheels caught in a ditch and the aircraft rolled, burned and killed all on board. Nothing was left except some gray powder and the engines. As scary as it was, I loved to fly the CH-34 and can still smell the odor of its exhaust in my mind.

Near the conclusion of this phase of our training we conducted three days of field exercises. My Vietnamese stick buddy and I flew together, taking turns flying as copilot for each other as we rotated the flying duties. During this exercise I experienced my first close brush with disaster.

Cadet An almost flew us into the ground while making a night landing. He put the aircraft in a flare (pulled the nose up) to slow it down and lost sight of the landing zone. He said nothing and I was looking out the side window. Suddenly I sensed that the ground coming up too fast. At the last second, I grabbed the controls, rolled in full throttle and pulled the collective all the way up. The wheels hit the ground and we bounced and lurched back into the air. We ended up at a high hover over some trees. I am sure the instructor on the ground was having a heart attack as he watched us slowly hover back to the landing pad.

After getting out of the aircraft and changing into a clean flight suit, I went to the instructor and told him I was through flying. He calmed me down and made me fly again that night with him. I never again trusted anyone else on the controls. This was to save me at least twice in the years to come.

About this time I learned a valuable lesson about unintended consequences. A flight of several CH-34s practicing low level formation flying managed to stray out of the training area and buzz a turkey ranch. Hundreds of turkeys were reportedly killed when they piled into the corner of a building while reacting to our loud engine and rotor noise. The Army had to pay for the damage and our instructors got into trouble.

Cadet An completed his advanced training and returned to Vietnam where he flew the CH-47 in combat. I only saw him there one time. After our visit he wrote Mary Jane a letter, telling her that I was safe. He also said we would win the war and I would be home soon. He got two out of three right.

We next learned to fly the UH-1 Huey. It was much easier to fly because it had hydraulic power assisted controls and a governor on the throttle that maintained a constant RPM. I remember the first time I picked it up to a hover. It seemed to be light, powerful and ready to leap into the air. We completed instrument and tactical training, and were introduced to air-to-ground gunnery in this phase. Not knowing that I would soon be flying gunships, I paid little attention aerial gunnery.

During this phase we lost one crew when a Huey fell apart in the air. In those days the aircraft was fairly new and maintenance problems were a constant threat to safety. You rolled the dice every time you went up. A favorite saying was to announce that we had 'cheated death again' at the conclusion of every flight.

A helicopter is inherently unstable. If you take your hands off of the controls it will kill you in less than a minute. Visualize yourself trying to sit on top of a football. Alternately, a fixed wing aircraft is inherently stable. If you take your hands off of the controls, it will pretty much fly itself. Visualize the stability of hanging from a parachute.

A helicopter will also kill you if you fly into a cloud, lose sight of the ground and fail to properly use the flight instruments. Therefore, I paid close attention to my instrument training. I knew that I would be playing for keeps if I ever found myself in a cloud. During our training we had one aircraft take off on a foggy morning and crash. I added the weather to all of the other things I had to worry about.

The Army was in a hurry to get us out of flight school so they only provided enough training on instrument flight procedures to get out of trouble. Later, after my first tour in Vietnam, I would return to the school to train for, and be issued an instrument rating. With this designation, I was qualified to could make a planned flight in the clouds without seeing the ground except at landing. The Army's failure to provide all new helicopter pilots with an instrument rating cost the lives a lot of good men in the next few years.

My next door neighbor while at Fort Rucker was a civilian and the director of a civilian airfield near Ozark. He owned a small fixed wing aircraft and offered to take me for a flight in it. This was my first introduction to flying a fixed wing aircraft. I knew instantly that this was something I had to learn to do, and at every opportunity in the future, asked the Army to send me to fixed wing school, which they finally did.

When we got airborne he gave me the controls and it was so easy to fly that I was sure I could master it with a couple of hours of training. I later found out that it was strictly against Army regulations for student pilots to fly civilian aircraft. If my instructors had caught me, I would have been kicked out of flight school.

Shortly before graduation, and when I was assured I would be getting flight pay (which was one hundred and twenty five Dollars, or about half of what I got for my base pay), we decided we could afford a new car. We traded the old station wagon for a sparkling new 1964 Chevrolet two door coupe. We also could afford to now buy some furniture. It initially looked good but could not stand up to the frequent Army moves. During our twenty six moves over the years we were to destroy a lot of furniture.

Flight pay became a recurring issue between my non-flying friends and me over the years. They were jealous, and would often say that pilots earned our flight pay, but not our base pay. It was technically named 'hazardous duty pay' and was justified because our life insurance was relatively expensive. That extra pay allowed my family to always live a little above the edge of poverty and to eventually own a home. Some of my friends decided to invest in stocks with all of their flight pay throughout their careers. If I had done that, I would have had a nice pot of money when I retired. Hindsight is always 20/20.

CHAPTER 3

PREPARING FOR WAR

I graduated near the top of my class and was offered the opportunity to volunteer for duty in Vietnam, which I turned down. Two of my classmates took the offer. Little did I know that about six months later I would join them, and all three of would end up in the same unit. One of them was badly wounded. The other completed his tour but was later killed in an aircraft training accident at Fort Sill, Oklahoma.

My orders took me to Fort Benning, Georgia and the 11th Air Assault Division, which had been formed to test the air assault concept. I was assigned to the 377th Aerial Rocket Artillery (ARA) Battalion. To my delight, this was considered to be a field artillery assignment.

There were two Army Divisions at Fort Benning at that time. One was the 11th and the other was the 2nd Infantry Division. Since the place was so crowded, we had to rent a house off post in Columbus, Georgia. Shortly after moving into our house a new neighbor moved in across the street. He had flown helicopters in Vietnam and invited us over to look at his photographs. It seemed that every other picture he showed us was a shot of him receiving a medal. He would smugly say "and here I am receiving another award." I was deeply impressed at the time, but later when I served in his old unit I found out that most of his awards were the type that were given for just being there.

I was a member of the ARA Battalion for only a short time, but my experience there stands out since it was my first operational flying assignment. The ARA was equipped with UH-1 Huey helicopters that were armed with rocket pods containing forty eight folding fin aerial rockets, half mounted on each side. The aircraft had a crew of four men including a pilot and copilot who were either officers or warrant officers. The crew chief and door gunner were enlisted men, and each manned a door mounted machine gun. This was to be the standard UH-1 Huey crew set-up for the entire Vietnam War.

During one of my first trips to the gunnery range I learned about target fixation during target attack. One of our pilots was firing rockets while diving on a target and kept firing until he flew directly into the target, killing the crew. The Air Force had known about this unexplained fatal problem with pilots since World War One. Army Aviation was learning the hard way. From that time on, I required my copilot to call out the altitude at one hundred feet intervals throughout a rocket run. I had learned my first of many practical lessons in attack helicopter employment techniques.

During this period the reconnaissance unit of the 11th Division was equipped with brand new OV-1 Mohawk aircraft. These twin engine fixed wing airplanes flew at about three hundred mph, and were designed to gather battlefield intelligence using wing mounted radar and infrared systems. However, some enterprising Army pilots decided to attach bombs and machine guns under their wings and turn them into ground attack close air support aircraft.

There was one big problem. Up until that time, most Army fixed wing pilots flew L-19 Bird Dog observation aircraft that cruised at about one hundred mph. They had no experience flying the fast, low level attack profile. Thus, the unit suffered several fatal wire strike and target fixation accidents in a short period of time. They simply were flying too fast and low for their proficiency level. The Mohawk became known as another 'Widow Maker.'

The Army started to use armed Mohawks in Vietnam in about 1964. The U.S. Air Force found out about it and complained to the Department of Defense. They saw the armed Mohawk as a threat to their traditional role of providing air to ground firepower. They claimed that the armed fixed wing aircraft mission belonged exclusively to them. The Department of Defense agreed and the Army was subsequently forced to disarm all Mohawks. For some reason the Air Force never complained about armament on helicopters.

A few weeks after arrival in my new unit I was asked to fill out a questionnaire relating to my previous assignments. The question that stood out was one that asked if I had served in Vietnam. When I checked the 'no' box, I somehow knew that I would be headed in that direction soon. Sure enough, about a week later the word came that I was being transferred to the 3d Aviation Company, a unit being formed at Fort Benning for deployment to Vietnam.

Mary Jane learned about my transfer before I did. I was in the field on a training exercise. The unit commander decided to call all the wives together and inform them as a group to prevent rumors. In addition, he said he did it so the women could get their crying over-with before we came home. That is exactly how it worked. They informed us in the field but did not tell us that the women had been informed. On the long helicopter ride home that day I was trying to figure a way to tell Mary Jane the bad news. When I walked in and before I could say anything, she said she knew. I do not remember seeing a tear from her until I actually got on the aircraft to depart. I had learned another valuable lesson in human relations and the power of preemption.

The unit to which I was assigned was organized into three platoons of eight aircraft and about sixteen pilots each. Commanded by Captains, two of the platoons were equipped with airlift helicopters and one with armed helicopters, all Hueys. The airlift platoons were assigned the UH-1D, which was a little bigger than the UH-1B armed version.

As our training progressed, I was forced to do more and more flying in formation with other helicopters. Our commander constantly pushed us to get closer and closer together. He wanted our rotor blades to overlap! His assertion was that the closer we flew, the more helicopters we could simultaneously get into a landing zone, thus putting more troops on the ground early in the battle. It went unsaid that another reason for flying so close together was that our attention would be so focused on holding our place in the formation we would not notice enemy gunfire.

One evening I watched a television program called 'Letters from Home.' It was about helicopters in combat in Vietnam. The unit featured in the film was an armed helicopter company. I could not help but notice that the helicopters, which carried machine guns and rockets, did not fly in formation. Rather, they flew with several hundred yards of separation between each aircraft. By flying spread out, they could quickly place rocket fire on the ground under someone else that was receiving gunfire. As I watched the program unfold it occurred to me that here was a way to escape having to fly in those fearful formations. All I had to do was change from flying airlift helicopters to flying armed helicopters. However, making this change would prove to be much more difficult than I imagined.

I asked for and got permission from my airlift platoon leader to talk to the armed helicopter platoon leader about the possibility of transferring to his 'guns.' He seemed receptive and asked me where I got my commission. I told him I was a product of the college ROTC program. He arrogantly informed me that he only wanted pilots who were former enlisted men with officer's candidate school commissions. The implication was that I was not good enough to fly in his platoon. Neither of us realized that in about nine month he would report to me in Vietnam and fly as my copilot on a combat mission. More about that a little bit later.

In November, 1964 we completed our training and were given thirty days leave to relocate our families. I moved Mary Jane and the children to Baxter, Tennessee, which was close to her parent's home. She was going to need some help while I was away. This was our fourth move in about a year and the strain was starting to show on all of us.

Later during my absence Bill, who was about three, reached onto the kitchen stovetop and pulled a pot of boiling beans over on him severely burning his arm. In another mishap Mary Jane had an automobile accident that knocked some of Nonna's front teeth out. To keep me from worrying, I was not told about these incidents until I returned. I found out about the auto accident when I questioned why the old Chevy was running down the road kind of sideways. The repair shop had been unable to get its frame straight.

I reported back to Fort Benning on 25 November 1964. The entire company departed the next day on a very uncomfortable U.S. Air Force cargo aircraft that had been equipped with troop seats. We stopped in Hawaii for fuel and spent the night. A few of us took a taxi into Honolulu and looked around. I concluded that Hawaii would be a nice place to live. Little did I know that I would ultimately live there for a total of fourteen years. After another overnight stop at Clark Airbase in the Philippines, we flew into Bien Hoa Airfield on 28 November and started the clock ticking on our one year combat tour.

Upon arrival in Vietnam, I was shocked to find out that our unit was to be broken up and distributed as individual replacements throughout the country. We traveled about twenty five miles by bus to Saigon and were gathered into a large room for the purpose of receiving our assignments. As you can imagine, there was a lot of apprehension among us as we contemplated our future. The personnel officer used a large map to show us the dozen or so locations throughout the country where helicopter units were located. He said we would be spread among all of these locations.

He explained that there was one unit in the country that was considered high risk, and was made up of volunteers only. He told us a little about the unit and I immediately recognized it as the one that was the subject of the television program 'Letters from Home' that I had seen a few months earlier. Here was my opportunity to get into a pure armed helicopter unit. No formation flying!

When he asked if there were any volunteers for the unit, I was the first to raise my hand. Three other officers also raised their hands. That is how Carl Mangold, Mike Hammer and Lyal Erwin ended up reporting with me that afternoon to the Utility Tactical Transport Helicopter Company (UTT) at Tan Son Nhut airfield in Saigon.

A few weeks before my arrival the UTT had been re-designated the 68th Armed Helicopter Company. That designation number would later be changed to the 197th and even later to the 334th. I never understood why the Army continuously changed unit designations. It was like someone was repeatedly stealing our identity. The pilots, however, maintained the spirit of the old UTT throughout all the changes and had an aggressive, elitist attitude throughout the war.

1964 era Playboy UH-1B Huey gunship. Note the heavy plastic that was placed in the lower part of the windshield to (hopefully) deflect bullets.

The UTT was truly the 'Lafayette Escadrille' of the Vietnam War. It had been activated in Okinawa in July, 1961. As the Army's first and only armed helicopter unit, it spent the next year developing weapons systems and training in the Philippines and in Thailand. On 9 October 1962 it deployed to Vietnam. It was equipped with the first UH-1 Huey helicopters to enter combat. The weapons systems were pretty much 'home made' since the Army was feeling its way into the armed helicopter business. Not only did the unit have to figure out how to arm the aircraft, it had to develop ways to employ them on combat operations.

Underbelly view of UH-1B gunship. The copilot controlled the machine guns. They were fed with hundreds of rounds of linked ammunition.

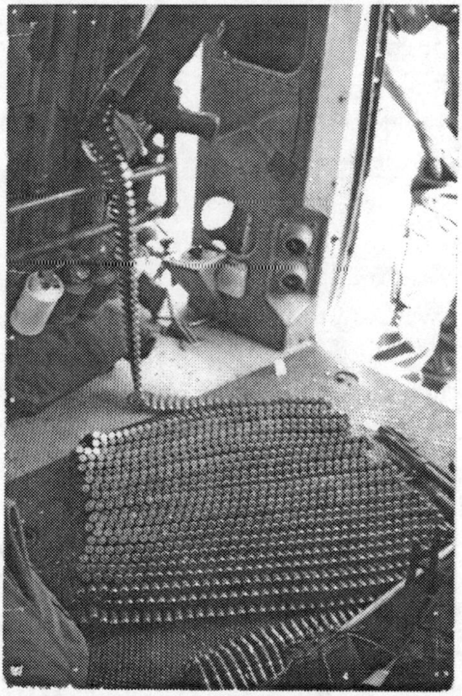

Linked door gunner ammunition carefully arranged so it would flow freely and continuously.

Kent Paxton in copilot seat behind the pull-down gun sight that controls the four machine guns. I am behind the rocket sight.

The UTT brought a new 'fighter helicopter' mentality to the battlefield. Their initial mission was to provide armed escort to the old and highly vulnerable CH-21 Ute. Over time and as the needs of the Vietnam battlefield changed, and as crew and aircraft capabilities were discovered and expanded, other missions were added as will be detailed later.

The company radio call sign was 'Saber.' Our two mottos were 'First with Guns' and 'We Lead the Way.' We had crossed sabers painted on the doors of our aircraft, which later disturbed the air cavalry units that were deployed when large American troop formations began to arrive. Crossed sabers are the symbol of the U.S. Cavalry. At that early time in the war however, we performed the air cavalry mission as well as all other armed helicopter missions in Vietnam.

When I arrived our aircraft were armed with four pedestal mounted 7.62 millimeter M-60 machine guns, two on each side. They could be pointed toward a target by the copilot using a hand held sight. In addition, the two door gunners each had a hand held M-60 that was suspended from the top of the passenger door on a rubber cord. Each of the M60s could fire at a rate of about five hundred rounds per minute. If all guns were simultaneously firing, there would be over three thousand rounds per minute going out. In addition, we carried on each side of the aircraft a pod of 2.75 inch folding fin aerial rockets. The capacity of the pods varied, but our normal load was seven rockets on each side. The rockets had a range of about one half mile. The high explosive warhead weighed ten pounds, which was about one forth as powerful as the round fired by the 105 millimeter howitzer used by field artillery units.

Over the course of the war the weapons systems and ammunition for helicopters was progressively improved and expanded. The high explosive warhead weight was increased to seventeen pounds. In addition, we eventually had a variety of warheads from which to choose. Some of the type's available included smoke, white phosphorus and armor piercing.

A key piece of ordinance that was central to our operations was the smoke hand grenade. As we flew over hostile territory, each door gunner held a smoke grenade with the safety pin almost pulled. At the first sound of enemy fire he pulled the pin, dropped the grenade out of the door, loudly announced on the intercom 'receiving fire' and gave the direction from which the bullets were coming. The pilot immediately turned away from the source of gunfire, the door gunners started firing their machine guns and the other aircraft in the flight fired rockets at the target. In seconds the smoke grenade was on the ground and we could direct additional fire relative to its position. This rush of action usually caused the enemy to duck long enough for us to get into position to fire a full load of ammunition on his position.

In order to fully understand many of the combat actions I am going to relate, you need to know a little about the way we employed our helicopters. In flight school we had been taught to simply fly up to a target, shoot it, and then fly away. However, when I got to Vietnam I found out that there was a lot more to it than that.

Our unit always flew with at least two helicopters in a flight. The lead aircraft was the 'fire team leader' and the second one was the 'wingman.' This was called a 'light' fire team, and was usually commanded by a Lieutenant. For especially tough missions a third aircraft would join the flight. That one was usually flown by the platoon leader, a Captain, and was equipped with a load of forty eight rockets and no flexible machine guns. This flight of three was known as a 'heavy fire team.'

There were good reasons for at least two aircraft flying on all of our missions. The primary one was that the wingman protected the lead aircraft while the team leader concentrated on performing the leadership and decision making functions. In addition, there was always a second helicopter there in case one of the team was shot down. The advantages to crew confidence and survivability are obvious.

As pointed out earlier, when the UTT arrived in country there was no such thing as armed helicopter tactics. I arrived two years later at just the right moment to take advantage of what the unit had learned through trial and error. Just before my arrival, a fire team leader who had survived his tour and was preparing to depart, Lieutenant J. A. Damron, was just finishing a booklet that recorded the very first set of tactical doctrine ever written for armed helicopters operating in Vietnam. It became affectionately known as the 12 Cardinal Rules of Attack Helicopter Combat.

Our gunner platoon leader, Lieutenant Jerry Walker (call sign 'Gunner Six') on left. He flew frequently as one of my door gunners

CHAPTER 4

THE CARDINAL RULES

Soon after arrival my new platoon leader gave me a twenty seven page typewritten booklet and told me that the twelve rules contained in it were the result of combat lessons learned. He pointed out that every rule came into being because someone made a mistake that cost lives or serious wounds. He also told that if I had any hopes of going home in one piece, I would learn and use these rules. Accordingly, I studied them carefully. Every mission I flew during the next year was guided by the rules. I am confident that they saved my life many times.

As a side note, at about the time I departed in 1965, aviation units began arriving in large numbers and going directly into battle. It appeared to me that they did not know about, or care about tactics or rules. Consequently, I believe many units suffered tremendous unnecessary casualties. The worst of these units were the air cavalry squadrons that deployed with the divisions. From what I observed on my later two tours, there was little effort made to learn from mistakes that others had already made. This is just one more reason I am thankful that I served my first tour in the UTT.

To set the stage for my later descriptions of combat actions, each of the rules is separately explained below. Keep in mind that there are true stories about combat casualties that go with each rule. I will relate many of them later.

1. Do not fly in the dead man zone without a reason. This zone is generally the airspace between fifty feet above the ground up to one thousand feet. It is the area where Vietcong had a good chance of hitting your aircraft. It had been found from captured documents that the Vietcong were trained to 'lead' a helicopter by aiming at a point about one helicopter length in front of it. Above one thousand feet of altitude, odds were that the lead would not be enough and he would shoot behind you. On the deck you were visible for only a short time and the enemy has little or no time to aim before firing, so his lead was usually not enough and again shot behind the aircraft. We tried to spend as little time as possible in the dead man zone.

2. Always make a high reconnaissance first. This rule went hand in hand with the one above. It may be hard to believe but we wanted the enemy to shoot at us. That was how we found him in about ninety five percent of the cases. Since we had a better chance of not getting hit at higher altitude, we always flew over the area at around twelve hundred feet before transitioning through the dead man zone to nap-of-the-earth (a few feet above the ground). Because of the extended range of the fifty caliber heavy machine gun, we moved this first pass up to about two thousand feet if we had any reason to suspect that the enemy had them in the area.

3. Never fly directly behind another aircraft. Known as the one hundred and eighty degree wing position, flying directly behind another aircraft could prove deadly. The first helicopter to fly over would alert the enemy who usually missed in his haste to fire. If the second aircraft was flying directly behind the first one, all the enemy gunner had to do was hold his original aim and he had a better chance of getting a hit. To prevent this, the wing man would fly at an angle of from twenty to forty five degrees off to the side of the lead aircraft. This angle was constantly changing as the wing man tried to stay in the best position to fire rockets under the lead if he received fire.

4. Never fly parallel to any feature. The enemy was usually deployed with an escape route at his back. Therefore, he would be located along the edge of the jungle, the shoreline of a river or a rice paddy dike. If we flew parallel to the feature, we were exposing our aircraft to the entire array of enemy firepower. Therefore, we tried to cross any linear feature at an angle and always in a turn.

5. Do not over-fly the target. If the area was considered a target it obviously contained the enemy, and we were shooting at it. This usually made the enemy very mad. They knew that their position had been located so they no longer tried to hide or hold fire. Also, if you were shot down over enemy positions you had no choice but to make an emergency landing almost directly below where you were flying. You definitely did not want to land in the middle of a bunch of mad guys with guns. Thus, we always broke off the attack short of the target and made a sharp turn one way or the other, usually toward friendly troops. This maneuver was called the 'break' and was planned in advance and announced on the radio by the fire team leader before the attack.

6. Always assume the area is hot. With no front lines the enemy could be anywhere, even just outside the gate of the airfield. We armed all our weapons systems before we took off and were ready to return fire as soon as we crossed the fence. One common mistake other units made later in the war was to assume that if one aircraft landed in an area safely, it was not hot. The enemy was very good at hiding and waiting until just the right time to start shooting. They often waited until before dark because they knew our night capability was limited and they had a better chance of escaping. For that reason, we simply dreaded any action late in the day.

7. Never fire until you have the friendly forces identified. The biggest fear of a gunship pilot was to fire on friendly troops,

especially Americans. We went out of our way to make sure we knew where all the friendly forces were located. This was done in one of two ways. If they had panel markers (pieces of orange cloth), they would place them on the ground in and around their area. The second and quickest way was to call for the friendly forces to throw smoke grenades. Since the enemy was known to monitor our radio frequencies, we would not tell the ground forces what color of smoke to deploy. If we did, the enemy could throw some too, and confuse us. Therefore, we let the friendly forces choose the color of smoke, throw it and after we got a good look at their positions, tell them what color we were seeing. To my knowledge, I never once shot up friendly forces, which is unfortunately not true for some of my contemporaries.

8. Avoid firing over the heads of friendly troops. At first glance, being over friendly forces when you fire sounds like a good idea. If you are shot down and can land within their lines, they can help you. However, there are a couple of good reasons for not firing over their positions. First, the enemy was usually oriented to fire at the ground forces so all they had to do to shoot at us was raise the barrel of their weapon up a bit, and there we were. Second, we dropped huge amount of expended machine gun cartridges and links as six machine guns fired. All that falling brass created control problems and confusion among the troops on the ground as they often thought they were being fired upon. To avoid this we would plan our attack to approach from the side at an angle of about forty five degrees. We would terminate the attack and make our break short of the friendly positions.

9. Fire only when you have a worthwhile target. The purpose of this one was to assure we did not waste our ammunition then suddenly need it on the way home. It was always a temptation to do some shooting in a free fire zone (area declared to be totally under enemy control) at the end of a mission in order to

keep our shooting skills sharp. However, in the environment of Vietnam, you never knew when you would suddenly receive fire from the ground and need to shoot your way out of the situation. Also, we were often called on the radio while flying home from a mission and re-directed to an emergency situation. These missions usually involved an outpost under attack, a downed aircraft or an emergency medical evacuation mission. A final reason for not shooting unless you needed to do so was that the machine guns and rocket launchers on each aircraft would have to be cleaned and reloaded at the end of the day, which would take the crew several extra hours.

10. Always know the situation. Knowing as much as possible about both the friendly and the enemy situation before arrival at the mission site was absolutely critical to success and survival. The most sought after information was related to the location and caliber of enemy antiaircraft weapons. We could usually deal with small arms but we could not compete with fifty caliber heavy weapons. Later in the war we also avoided at all costs the shoulder fired SA-7 anti-aircraft guided missiles. An equally important piece of information was the exact location of all friendly forces so we would not accidentally shoot them up. There was nothing more feared than to receive a radio call during a firing pass instructing you to break off the attack because you were shooting up friendly troops. Therefore, while flying to a mission site we would constantly be working the radios trying to glean any tidbit of information available.

11. Brief your elements to a man. Since any member of a crew could get shot at any time, everybody needed to know as much about the situation as the mission commander. This knowledge would help the surviving crewmembers take the proper action to resolve what was often a critical situation. I recall a crew that was shot down without knowing the location of friendly and enemy forces. Upon getting out of the crashed aircraft they

mistakenly moved toward the enemy forces, which resulted in unnecessary casualties.

12. Take your time. When people are screaming on the radio that they are being shot to pieces, there is a strong temptation to jump into the fight as quickly as possible. To do so could cause you to violate several of the above rules, and could result in worsening the situation by shooting up friends or being shot down yourself. This is one lesson I learned the hard way early in my tour when I directed my door gunners to fire on a target without knowing we were flying directly over a friendly patrol. The falling empty brass shells panicked the patrol leader and he thought we were shooting at him. He called us all kinds of names on the radio, which was heard by other crews operating nearby on the same radio frequency. My name was mud until the ground troops figured out what had happened and apologized. From then on, I took my time.

You will notice that the 13th Cardinal Rule is missing. It was not one of the original rules, and did not exist at the time of my arrival in the unit. I developed it on my very first day of combat operations, as I will detail shortly. Fittingly, rule thirteen was to be the one most responsible for my survival of over one thousand armed helicopter combat missions.

During any discussion regarding armed helicopter tactics one of the first questions I get asked is: "did you get shot down?" The answer is yes but this is a more complex issue for a helicopter pilot than it is for a fixed wing driver. The fixed wing guys almost always lose their aircraft in a shoot-down, but the helicopter pilot has the capability to land in one piece because of his ability to zero out the forward speed of the aircraft at touchdown.

Most helicopter shoot-downs occur because a vital system, such as the fuel system or the oil supply, is shot out. This results in engine failure and a forced landing. For the fixed wing pilot the standard procedure is to 'punch out' and ride the parachute safely to the ground. Unfortunately, helicopter crews do not have this option because they are not equipped with parachutes. The Army had decided that there would not be time for helicopter crewmen to parachute out of a helicopter. Our only option was to fly the aircraft to the ground and land it in as few pieces as possible. I know of several fatal accidents and shoot-downs that would have been survivable for some or all of the crew had they been equipped with parachutes.

Since the helicopter can safely land almost anyplace where there is a clear, flat area, it is standard practice to land and 'check out' any suspected serious combat damage. This is called a 'precautionary landing,' and is not considered a shoot-down unless the aircraft is not capable of further flight without repairs. Using these rules, I concluded that I was shot down about seven times during my first year in Vietnam.

About a year after I returned from my tour with the UTT, I was asked by then Major Dick Jarrett to become a member of the AH-1G Cobra New Equipment Training Team (NETT). I accepted, and ended up deploying with the team to Vietnam where we introduced the new gunship into combat. During that year I was honored to be the team's tactics instructor. I used the Cardinal Rules as the basis for classes presented to the first several hundred Army Aviators who received transition training.

This was not the last time I was to teach younger aviators about the Cardinal Rules. In 1984, as a Colonel, I was selected to organize and train the Army's first light combat aviation brigade in the 7th Infantry Division at Fort Ord, California. Our mission was to prepare to fight and win in a low intensity environment (insurgency or with little or no armored forces). I taught classes on the Cardinal Rules to the aviators in the brigade, and incorporated the concepts into our training. After my departure the 7th successfully participated in combat operations in Panama. I like to think that a few lives were saved by the rules.

In 1987, while serving as Chief of Staff of the 101st Airborne Division (Air Assault), I participated in discussions on the Cardinal Rules with some groups of aviators. At that time the Army was still focused on a battle in Europe so the rules were less applicable than at other times. However, as the cold war faded away and our Army became engaged in the insurgencies in Iraq and Afghanistan, the rules regained their relevance. I hope someone is still teaching them.

CHAPTER 5

RUDE AWAKENINGS

With that introduction to my unit, our aircraft and tactics, I will describe the sequence of events surrounding my arrival in the UTT and my pre-combat checkouts. After a few hours of turning in records and drawing equipment my three friends and I were further assigned to one of the unit's three platoons. I have no idea how the decision was made that divided us up among the platoons. I went to the First Platoon, call sign 'Playboy,' and as I recall, Carl Mangold and Lyal Erwin to the Second Platoon call sign 'Raider.' Mike Hammer may have been assigned to the Third Platoon call sign 'Dragon.' In addition to the crossed sabers on the pilot's doors, all of the company helicopters had a distinctive platoon symbol painted on the nose. Our platoon's symbol was a white bunny head that looked like something out of the Playboy Magazine.

While in the flight operations building I experienced my first exposure to an operational mission. I overheard some excited radio traffic and a fire team landed and began quickly reloading with fuel and ammunition. From the stressed look on the crew's faces, it was clear that they were involved in a grave situation. The leader, a tall blond Captain, rushed into the building. I overheard him report that a Vietnamese fighter aircraft had been shot down north of Saigon. An American that had been on board had parachuted out and the team was going to try to rescue him (as I recall they were successful). I was impressed with this leader's business-like manner and the determination in his voice. As it turned out, he was Captain Dick Jarrett, the Playboy Platoon Leader, and my new boss.

At the end of the day I was taken to our living quarters where I was in for a big surprise. The unit officers lived in a rented Vietnamese villa (small hotel) just outside the gate of the airfield. The enlisted men and non-commissioned officers lived on the airfield near our flight line. The villa was three stories high, had a kitchen, dining room, bar, patio and vehicle parking area. There were a couple of other villas inside the compound. The entire complex was surrounded by a concrete wall and guarded by Vietnamese civilians that were employed by the unit.

I was assigned to a small bedroom that I was to share for several months with Chief Warrant Officer Kent Paxton. A short energetic man with an infectious smile, he immediately got my attention by announcing that his previous roommate (and the former occupier of my new bed) had been seriously wounded a couple of days earlier and evacuated to Japan. I soon discovered that Kent had a great reputation as a combat pilot and was considered to be the best navigator in the company. He would prove to be highly instrumental in my development into an effective member of the unit.

The first evening after I arrived at my new home I was taken to downtown Saigon to 'Cheap Charlie's.' This was the unit's favorite Vietnamese store for purchasing uniforms and equipment needed to supplement the items issued by the Army. I was told to purchase some uniforms and hats with all of the insignia embroidered on them, and a western style pistol holster with ammunition pouches for the forty five caliber pistol I was to be issued.

When it came time to pay for the items, I got a better deal than I expected. I still had some American money. Charlie gave me one hundred and twenty Piasters (Vietnamese money) for each dollar. The official exchange rate at that time was about eighty Piasters per dollar, so I got about thirty percent more for my money than I would have if I had exchanged my money at an American facility. A few months later the U.S. Military made it illegal for any American in Vietnam to possess real dollars. We were then issued 'script dollars,' which looked something like Monopoly Money. This funny money was used until the end of the war.

We arrived back at the villa from our shopping trip to find the off-duty pilots gathered on the patio having a few drinks and shooting rats. Yes, shooting big fat rats. The weapon of choice was a crossbow, and the rats were running around in a drainage ditch outside the wall of the compound. The crossbow was a souvenir that had been obtained by one of the crews while on a mission to support a Montagnard tribe in the highlands. This unique entertainment had been developed because the bored pilots were on call for emergency missions and therefore restricted to the villa.

Rat shooting was to continue nightly until the arrows ran out. That night Captain Gene Fudge, an outgoing Texan with a taste for Jack Daniels whiskey and Days Work chewing tobacco, took out his twelve gage sawed off and chrome plated shotgun and started blasting rats. The noise of the gunshots triggered the attack alarm. We were soon surrounded by Vietnamese and American Police. Needless to say, our commander insisted we find a new form of amusement following that event.

My next exposure to the seriousness of my situation came the next day when I reported to the flight line to start in-country training. The helicopters looked like they had the measles. They had small metal patches at various places. My curiosity faded to horror when I realized that each spot covered a bullet hole. Some comfort was gained when further inspection revealed that flack jackets had been placed under the helicopter's seats, thick plastic strips had been installed on the lower part of their windshields, and there were metal plates attached inside their doors.

I was advised by Warrant Office Bobby Smith, the platoon instructor pilot, to fly with my pistol between my legs in position to protect my private parts. When issued this pistol, I had been told that its primary purpose was to destroy my helicopter if it was shot down in enemy territory (fondly known as 'shooting your horse'). I was issued six tracer rounds that were to be fired into the fuel tank. It was becoming increasingly clear that I was about to embark on deadly serious business.

Another indicator that I was in a whole new situation came when I asked one of the pilots about the presence of dozens of bicycles on the flight line. The ground crewmen were zooming about in all directions on these bicycles. He told me that the unit patrolled several roads that were closed to all traffic. Anyone found on these roads was considered enemy. In many cases a person on the roads would hear a helicopter coming, drop their bicycle, and disappear into the jungle. One of the aircraft would then land and 'take possession' of the enemy equipment. Landings to pick up enemy gear was soon stopped by our commander when a crew from another unit got shot up while making an approach to retrieve an enemy flag that was flying from a tree top.

All pilots that report to a new unit must undergo a check ride to demonstrate their level of proficiency with the machine. This is particularly important when joining a unit in a combat zone. After this flight the unit instructor pilot sets up a training program designed to bring the new arrival up to unit standards and to teach procedures particular to that unit. My training program consisted of several hours of individual study of maps and operating procedures, and about three hours of flying with the instructor. We focused on making emergency landings and on gunnery practice at a nearby training area.

The training area turned out to be not so friendly. During a firing pass we received some small arms fire and a hole was shot in a hydraulics line. We immediately lost boost (power steering) to the flight controls and had to make an emergency landing. After this 'realistic training' I felt ready to go and my instructor must have felt the same way because he cleared me for operational flying starting the next day.

I got off to a real shaky start that morning when my alarm clock didn't work. One of the pilots stuck his head in the door of my room, woke me and said I had ten minutes to report to the truck that would carry us to the airfield. There would be no time to shave and no breakfast. Worse, the Vietnamese cleaning crew had removed all of my uniform shirts to wash them. I awoke my roommate and quickly explained the problem. He loaned me one of his shirts. However, he wore a small size and I needed a medium. The sleeves would not button and left uncovered about 6 inches of my arms. It dawned on me that I would be a laughing stock if I showed up in this little shirt with its Warrant Officer rank and somebody else's nametag. The only way out, I reasoned, was to cover the shirt by putting on my flack jacket, which was normally carried to the airfield and put on only when you got in the aircraft. By solving one problem I created another one.

There were eleven other crewmembers on the mission that day. All of them closely observed me to determine how I would perform on this first mission. I later found out that they were a little suspicious when I wore the flack jacket on the truck ride and throughout the preflight briefing and aircraft checks. They became more suspicious when I did not take it off during routine refueling stops later in the morning, even though we were in a secure area and the temperature was getting hot. My reputation would probably have been forever soiled had we not engaged an enemy force late in the afternoon.

We received a radio report that a group of Vietcong soldiers had attacked a village south of Saigon and were fleeing. We flew to the designated area and on the high recon our flight leader spotted three armed men running along a rice paddy dike. Our mission commander that day was the platoon leader, Captain Jarrett. He radioed an attack command that was to become a classic. He said: "three men on a dike, kill them, break right."

Since there was suspicion that I might be some kind of 'chicken,' a decision was made to let me do the shooting. I was flying as copilot and had in my hands the handles of a sight that directed the four interconnected machine guns mounted on flexible mounts. As the pilot descended toward the men on the dike, I pulled the trigger and the guns started to fire. I became fixated on the target. I continued to hold the triggers down as we got closer and closer. Finally the pilot yelled at me: "cease fire, cease fire." I released the triggers just as we passed a few feet above the ground. The air was filled with mud and lots of other stuff and it splattered all over the windshield.

As I came back to my senses, I decided I was now in real trouble. In flight school this mistake would surely have gotten me a pink slip for shooting too close to the target. However, this was not flight school. I had gone from goat to combat veteran. That night word went out that the Playboys had a new pilot that was so bloodthirsty he almost shot himself down. I never did tell anybody different.

My first day of flying combat missions did not end with the splattered windshield. After we landed, refueled and cleaned our aircraft, we were ordered to fly over a village called Binh Gia, which is about twenty five miles southeast of Saigon, to determine if there was any truth to a report that the Vietcong were occupying it. We flew to the area and descended to tree top level to make a fast pass over the buildings of the village.

I was flying as copilot in the second of three aircraft, and just as we cleared the village to the east, I heard several sounds from the rear of the aircraft. This was immediately followed by the pilot transmitting on the radio: "receiving fire – three o'clock" and both door gunners opened fire with their machine guns. Simultaneously there were several loud pops behind me, and explosions erupted on the ground below. The flight turned hard left, accelerated and started to climb.

The pops that I heard were the door gunners pulling the pins out of smoke grenades and tossing them out the door. I had not yet acquired an ear for the sound of bullets passing close by, so I did not identify the enemy rounds. The explosions under us were rockets launched by Captain Jarrett, who was flying behind the fire team. These rounds caused the enemy gunners to duck long enough for us to start our escape. We continued to receive fire for several seconds as we departed the area. It was during this short period of time that I first heard and recognized the sound of bullets going by and hitting the aircraft.

As we flew back to our home base I thought back on this short but intense action. It occurred to me that the combination of our turn, climb and increase in ground speed had tripled the enemy gunner's aiming problem. I searched my mind to relate this to the Cardinal Rules. It was not there. I had discovered what was to become my own personal 13th Cardinal Rule. Here it is.

13. Whenever possible, simultaneously keep the aircraft in a slight turn, a slight climb or descent, and constantly change airspeed. This maneuver gives the enemy gunner an almost impossible marksmanship problem. To achieve an aimed hit he has to effectively lead the aircraft in all three directions. Although the

> maneuver sounds complicated, it is relatively simple to accomplish. Any turn decreases the size of the effective rotor disk and induces a descent (a helicopter trying to fly on its side would have zero effective rotor disk). Rolling out of a turn has the opposite effect. Any raising or lowering of the nose produces a climb or descent, and lowers or raises the airspeed, all respectively. Therefore, the entire maneuver is controlled by slight movements of the cyclic, and after a few minutes of practice, is accomplished without conscious thought. The enemy's only recourse is to fire in the general direction of the aircraft and depend on luck for a hit.

At Bien Gia we had accomplished our mission by confirming that the enemy was there in large numbers. It was almost dark so we departed the area for our home base. Little did we know that our discovery would in a few days produce the biggest battle to date in Vietnam.

As the only armed helicopter company in country at that time, our firepower was in great demand. The company's mission required it to be available to support any battle anywhere in Vietnam. We could be dispatched on a moment's notice. Most assault helicopter companies had armed helicopter platoons they used to support their airlift platoons. However, those gunships generally did not support other operations. American fighter aircraft had not yet been authorized for use in Vietnam. When a serious fight occurred anywhere, we got involved. Thus, near the end of December 1964, and with little notice, a Playboy heavy fire team was ordered to proceed north to Da Nang to support a U.S. Marine CH-34 company.

In preparation for the trip we studied the maps and discovered one leg of the trip was longer than we could make with our two hours fuel supply. We requested the U.S. Air Force drop several fifty five gallon drums of fuel at a French rubber plantation along our route. We took hand pumps along and after a short search, found the fuel. It took about two hours to pump about one hundred gallons into each of the three aircraft. I often wondered what we would have done if we had not found that fuel.

After completing the hot job of pumping fuel we were glad to get back in the air and climb to altitude where it was cooler. Generally the temperature gets two degrees cooler for every one thousand feet you climb. As I recall, we climbed to four thousand feet above the ground. As we flew on to the north the temperature got cooler, so I allowed the gunners to slide their doors closed. We were approaching the city of Quy Nhon on the coast and were enjoying a splendid view of the ocean when there occurred one of those moments of stark terror that interrupts the usual boredom associated with flying from one point to the next.

There was a click and a pop from the back seat and suddenly, everything went white. I could not even see the end of my nose. One of the gunners had accidentally dropped a white smoke grenade in the floor of the helicopter and the safety pin had fallen out. This was cause for immediate panic because without constant reference to the horizon or the attitude indicator on the instrument panel, we would roll upside down and be chopped to pieces as we fell through our own rotor blades. As explained earlier, a helicopter, unlike a fixed wing aircraft, is inherently unstable and requires constant control inputs to keep it flying level. I somehow reacted with the only possible solution that would save us.

I kicked hard on the right tail rotor pedal and simultaneously opened my window. The tail rotor input forced the aircraft to slew and start to fly somewhat sideways. This directed wind into my window and blew the smoke out the gunner's door, which he had immediately opened to kick the burning grenade out. I got my head out the window and visually picked up the horizon as the aircraft rolled on its side. With this action I was able to regain control until the grenade was gone and all the smoke cleared.

Fortunately, I was flying at the back of the formation and the other crews never knew of this incident. If there had been an aircraft behind me he would have followed standard operating procedures and immediately fired rockets under my aircraft when the smoke grenade came out. We were flying over a village so no telling what kind of damage would have been done. I was learning lessons fast but learning them the hard way. Unfortunately, this was not the last hard lesson I would learn during the trip.

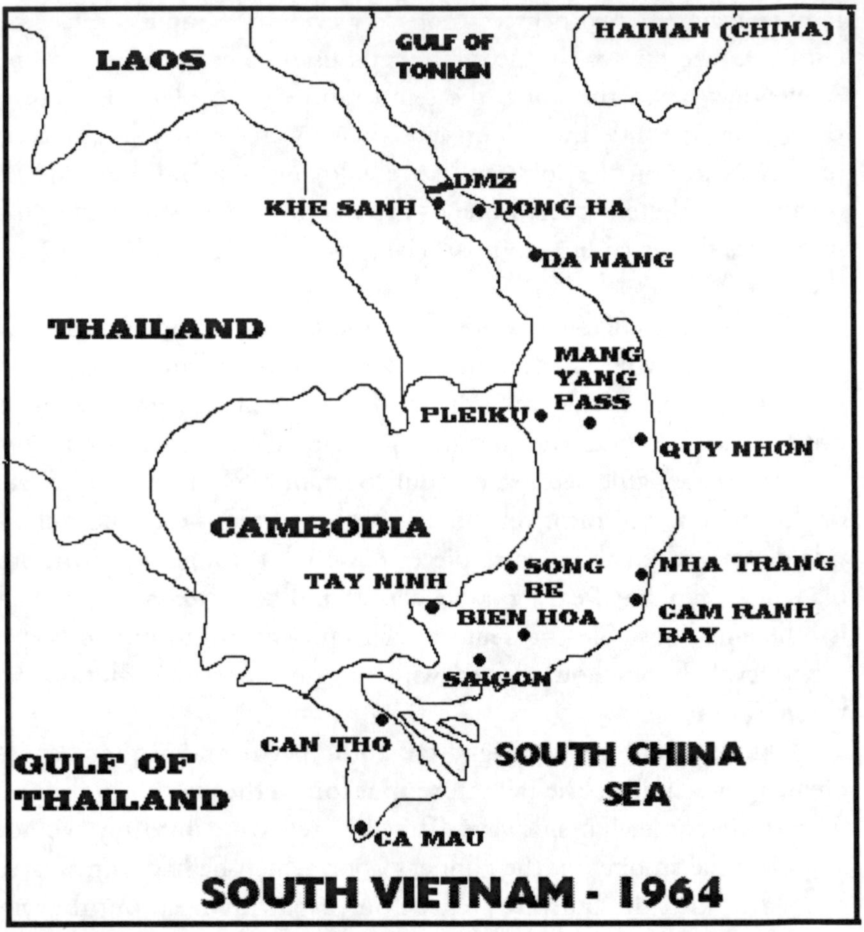

South Vietnam was a long thin country that stretched about six hundred miles from Ca Mau in the South to Dong Ha in the north. The terrain from Saigon south was almost all rice paddies with numerous rivers. North of Saigon rolling hills gradually turned into high mountains. I flew out of Saigon on my first tour, Bien Hoa on the second and Can Tho on the third.

Arriving at the Da Nang airfield late in the day, we found very little American presence. We landed alongside the runway and were directed to a parking space. After a long wait a military pickup truck came and transported us to the Grand Hotel in the downtown area. There were no Army facilities in that part of the country at that time. The hotel was a two story French affair built around a courtyard. I was assigned a downstairs room, which must have had fifteen feet ceilings. The room was damp and there was only one small light bulb. The single bed had a mosquito net hanging over it.

In the bathroom I found a shower and two commodes. I had never seen or heard about a French bathroom so was puzzled when I noticed one commode flushed, and the other squirted water upward. I found out later that the French do not use toilet paper but clean themselves with water. Live and learn.

Before we departed Saigon we were so involved that we had no time to think about Christmas. I had been receiving some gift packages from my family but had not opened them, deciding to honor the family tradition of saving gifts for opening on Christmas morning. I woke up, dumped my duffel bag of gifts on the bed and slowly opened them. It was the loneliest day of my young life. I had expected our crews to get together and celebrate Christmas in some fashion, but it was never mentioned and as a new guy, was not about to ask any questions.

Fortunately, we had some entertainment scheduled later in the day. I was looking forward to seeing The Bob Hope Show that was performing at the airfield that afternoon. While we were getting ready to go to the big show I was informed that I was suddenly considered qualified to command a fire team. My first mission in that capacity was to fly overhead cover during the performance. So much for seeing the show!

My wingman that day, and for most of the following year, was Chief Warrant Officer Jim Lee. He was a tall, trim young man who looked like he should still be in high school. However, he flew with the skill and determination of a veteran of much more experience. He possessed and frequently displayed an innate ability to anticipate enemy positions and often had rockets on target before I could complete my radio call announcing "receiving fire." He surely saved my life several times.

During my briefing for the mission I was informed that intelligence had reported a threat of a mortar attack. I was instructed to lead my team in big circles around the airfield throughout the performance. From one thousand feet overhead and about a mile away I could see the stage and the crowd but was not close enough to see any details. I tuned our navigation radio to a station that was playing Christmas music in order to participate in some small way in the celebration.

Downtown Da Nang 1964. My Wingman Jim Lee maintains a perfect thirty degree wing position on me even on the ground. Note lack of cars.

About halfway through the show I was called on the radio and directed to a location about five miles south of the airfield. There was a report that the enemy was setting up mortars. Upon arrival, I circled the area and suddenly, some enemy soldiers started shooting at my aircraft out of a clump of trees. I unloaded rockets and machine gun fire on the target and the shooting stopped. I must have ruined their day because there was no mortar attack. Years later I saw a video tape of that specific performance and at one point I am sure I heard helicopter rotor blades popping in the background. I always wondered if my rocket fire alarmed Bob and his group.

As stated earlier, our platoon's primary mission in Da Nang was to fly escort for a group of U.S. Marine CH-34 helicopters as they transported Vietnamese troops into battle. Our first job was to go to the landing zone before the transport aircraft arrived and fly high then low over the area to see if we could draw some enemy fire. If we did receive fire the airlift was delayed and we attacked the targets or called for artillery support. Then we would go back and start all over and repeat the process until there was no more enemy fire.

Occasionally we would arrive early and attack a landing zone even if we had not received fire. This was done if there was particularly good intelligence that the enemy was present. These types of attacks were called 'pre-strikes.'

Once the enemy was neutralized, or if none fired, we would join the troop carriers and get slightly behind them so we could return any fire they might receive. As the troop carriers slowed to land, we would fire into the tree and bushes on either side of them to keep the enemy's heads down. While they unloaded their troops, we would circle around and get into position to provide fire support as the troop carriers departed. After they were gone we usually stayed around to provide fire support for the ground troops as they engaged the enemy. This is generally how all helicopter assault missions unfolded.

Over the next few days we supported several air assaults and fired lots of ammunition. In fact, we used almost all of the rockets in the Da Nang ammunition dump. The local commander said we had expended his entire quarterly allocation, and he could not get more for weeks. Captain Jarrett called our Company Commander, Major Jim Jaggers, and asked him to get an emergency supply of rockets to us. A fast thinking, highly respected leader, Jim was well connected with the logistical staff in Saigon. He succeeded in getting a C-130 cargo airplane load of ammunition to us the next day. Thus, we were able to continue our mission without having to ration rockets.

About a week after Christmas my fire team was given a mission to fly up to the northwest corner of the country to a place named Khe Sanh. It was to become famous later in the war for the major battle that was fought there. We took off and climbed to about five thousand feet and crossed two mountain ranges. There were no roads, clearings or open spaces below us. We referred to this kind of flying as 'hanging our rear end on Lycoming.' Lycoming was the company that built our aircraft engine and if it failed on a trip like this, we would have no chance to land safely. Someone said that if we did go down, we might as well get a Montagnard wife and settle down because there was no way we would ever get out.

Major (later Major General) Joseph N. 'Jim' Jaggers, Jr. commanded the Company for the first half of my tour.

As we approached the airstrip at Khe Sanh we received small arms fire. I circled and landed to find the Vietnamese troops shooting artillery. There was a burned out transport aircraft beside the runway. I knew that we were in Indian country for sure. The American advisor came out to my aircraft and briefed me on the mission. He gave me a map with a grease pencil line drawn on it depicting the route to be flown. Along the route he had drawn little circles around points of interest at which he wanted me to look closely.

The American advisor and a Vietnamese observer flew in my aircraft to call for artillery if I needed it. They would also give me clearance to fire if I found a target. If fired upon first, I did not need clearance to fire back. These rules were laid out in a set of rules of engagement previously provided to me by my chain of command. Thus, I embarked on what was the first of many area reconnaissance missions I would fly during the next eleven months.

To accomplish an area reconnaissance I would lead the team up to about twelve hundred feet above the ground so I could accurately navigate along the route to the first area of interest. Upon arrival, I would carefully plan my approach by considering probable enemy locations, the wind direction and speed and the layout of the terrain. After a high pass I would descend down to treetop level, always in a turn, and if possible, approach with the wind and the sun at my back. I usually didn't see anything but trees and grass because the Vietcong were experts at camouflage. As a result, what I was really trying to accomplish was to get shot at. If I did, I would return fire to disengage and back off so the American advisor could call in artillery. If we were out of artillery range, I would attack the targets with our weapons.

On this particular mission we were fired upon from an enemy bunker complex. In response we dumped our rockets and rained intense machine gun fire onto the area. The enemy stopped shooting but I did not go in for a close look at the results. To do that after having fired most of our ammunition would have been foolish. The advisor called for artillery fire and I made a radio report detailing our progress, then flew back to the base to get more ammunition and fuel.

Keeping track of the status of fuel and ammunition was a key responsibility of the fire team leader. Our standard operating procedure called for me to plan missions for about one and one half hours flight time. That would leave us with a small reserve in case of an emergency. I had to constantly watch our fuel status and the estimated flying time to the refuel point. As you may be beginning to see, my job required almost constant thought and planning. In addition to keeping track of fuel and ammunition, I had to fly the aircraft, read a map, navigate, talk on several radios, keep track of my wingman and accomplish the tactical mission. Although I had a copilot to help me, I was usually so busy I had no time to think about getting shot.

We used a lot of ammunition. Here Lieutenant Jim Moody stands by an overfull container of empty M60 machine gun ammunition boxes.

Every night the platoon was in Da Nang Captain Jarrett placed a telephone call back to our headquarters in Saigon to give them a report on our activities. On the night of 30 December 1964 I was with him when he called. I noticed a sudden change in his tone of voice. It sounded like he was receiving some bad news.

There was a big fight in progress at the town of Binh Gia where I had received my baptism in enemy fire only a few days earlier. Several aircraft had been shot down. One was hit in the fuel tank and started burning. Before the crew could get it on the ground the entire tail boom came off. This made the aircraft fatally nose heavy and it dove into the ground killing all four crewmembers. This pilot had disregarded several Cardinal Rules and paid with his and his crew's life.

The battle started when the enemy ambushed a South Vietnamese column of armored personnel carriers that were moving into the area to check out our earlier report of enemy activity. The carriers had been caught and destroyed in a rubber plantation. An American advisor with the ground forces tried to escape into the forest. He had a handheld radio with which he kept up a running conversation with the helicopters overhead. Several helicopter crews tried frantically to locate and rescue him but he was either killed or captured, and was never heard from again. Another adviser in the same situation was rescued by one of our Raider platoon aircraft. Two more aircraft were lost, another pilot killed and several crewmembers seriously wounded.

The enemy had removed the fifty caliber machine guns off of the destroyed Vietnamese personnel carriers and used them to set up an ambush for our helicopters. At this point in the war there were very few of these heavy caliber guns available to the enemy. Our 7.62 millimeter guns and 3.75 inch rockets were no match of these weapons. We went out of our way to avoid getting in a fight with them. Their tactic was to position three guns in a triangle about one thousand yards apart. When we tried to attack one of them, the other two would have clear shots at us. During the remainder of the Vietnam War, armed helicopters encountering the fifty caliber bigger guns would usually back off and call in U.S. Air Force or Navy fighter-bombers.

Needless to say, we were pretty shook up about losing an entire crew. I had only been in country about three weeks at that point, and we had already lost two aircraft and one crew. I did not know any of those that were killed, but one of the badly injured pilots was a flight school classmate, 1Lt Paul Murray. He had been in the unit about five months, and was evacuated to the U.S. with burns and a broken foot. He was the first of many of my fellow flight school classmates to get wounded or killed in the war.

Two of the lost aircraft belonged to the Raider Platoon. After the first one was shot down, the second one tried to go in to help rescue the downed crew. However, it was shot up in the attempt. This resulted from our standing procedure that when a company aircraft went down, the next one closest to it would go in and try to help. There was always a fear that this would someday result in getting every last aircraft shot down, each trying to help the crew of the one before it. To my knowledge, the most to ever end up on the ground in this way was three aircraft. It was extremely reassuring to know that if you did go down, someone would be there to try to help.

As a platoon, we felt some responsibility for the loss of the aircraft and crewmembers at Binh Gia. They had been fighting a battle that we had started and we felt that we should have been there to help carry the load. Over the next month thousands of South Vietnamese troops were air assaulted into Binh Gia, and several more aircraft were shot down. One more pilot was killed by gunfire on 9 February.

After about three weeks of operations in and around Da Nang we were relieved by another platoon and flew back to our home base in Saigon. I am sure the Army support unit at Da Nang was glad to see us go. When we departed they were busy unpacking and assembling a new supply of rockets. Their parting comment was that our daily ammunition requirements exceeded what would otherwise be a month's supply for them.

Door gunner's hot spent machine gun brass routinely rained on pilots head and spilled down inside his shirt.

The Binh Gia operation finally ended in mid-February 1965. The town was cleaned out and returned to friendly hands. Our company had lost five killed and fourteen wounded. The unit was awarded a Distinguished Unit Citation for its action. For the remainder of my time in Vietnam, I never again flew near that place without misgivings.

CHAPTER 6

LEARNING THE HARD WAY

Shortly after our return to home base, on 15 January 1965, I was flying a mission just south of Saigon when I received a radio call that a Raider Platoon aircraft had gone down killing two crewmembers. Lost were my fellow volunteer Captain Lyal Erwin and his door gunner. They had been on a convoy escort mission north of town. The other two crewmembers survived. Lyal's aircraft had flown into an electrical transmission wire and crashed. This was not considered a combat loss but an accident.

During this period in Army Aviation history wires strikes were replacing mid-air collisions to become the helicopter pilot's worst nightmare. The problem existed not so much in Vietnam, which had only a few wires, but in our country and in Europe where most of the helicopter training was conducted close to the ground (nap-of-the- earth). Over my career, I probably lost more friends to wire strikes than to enemy action. A few years later the Army equipped all helicopters with wire cutting saw blades that were mounted above and below the windshield. These devices saved dozens of lives and are still, second to good eyeballs, the best defense against wires. However, they are not foolproof, and the military Services and civilians continue to lose crews and aircraft to wires.

Sometime in January 1965 the need for unarmed (slick) helicopters exceeded the number available. A decision was made to assign some routine supply missions to our unit. This required removal of the guns from one platoon's aircraft for a few weeks. The de-arming of our gunships was called 'slicking out.' The Company Commander, Major Jaggers decided to assign this mission the third, or Dragon Platoon. This event became known as the great 'Dragon slick out' and was the subject of a lot of trash talking by those of us who retained our guns. Gun pilots looked down on slick drivers like a sports car driver looks down on a truck driver, which is a pretty good analogy.

A few days later, and to my dismay, I was assigned a mission to fly a Dragon slick to supply ammunition to an outpost. I flew the aircraft a few miles east of Saigon to a Vietnamese district headquarters to pick up the ammunition. Upon arrival, a group of Vietnamese troops started loading the ammunition under the supervision of my crew chief. I did not notice that they were stacking all of it directly behind the pilot and copilot seats. I checked on the total weight and confirmed that it was well within our capability to lift, so gave it no thought, cranked up and took off. I had just made a serious and almost deadly mistake.

One of the most critical characteristics of a single rotor helicopter is maintaining its weight distribution within its center of gravity limitations. That is, the weight must be pretty well equalized on all sides of the single rotor or the aircraft will be out of balance and quickly become uncontrollable. Think of what happens when one person jumps off of a seesaw with the other person still in their seat and in the air. Not only is total weight important, but the location of the weight is equally critical. Again, think of the seesaw and visualize the outcome if one of the riders moved halfway up the board toward the pivot point.

As I pulled the aircraft off of the ground I tried to bring it to a stationary hover. However, I immediately found that even with full aft pressure on the cyclic stick, I could not keep the aircraft from accelerating forward. If the engine had died at that point, or if I had only a few more pounds behind the seats, we would have all been dead. As the aircraft passed through about sixty miles an hour, and with full aft cyclic still applied, I was ready to panic. For some reason I started a turn. This stopped the nose from going any further down, so the situation stabilized. By that time I had figured out what was wrong. I told the crew chief to start moving boxes of ammo back or throw some out. He moved a few toward the back of the helicopter, and I was able to get enough control to make a running landing in an open field nearby.

Once on the ground, I shut off the engine to let my blood pressure return to normal. We reloaded the ammunition closer to the center of gravity (back of the aircraft) and completed our mission without incident. This was my one and only slick mission, and it strongly reinforced my conviction that I belonged in guns. Because of this brush with disaster, I remained acutely aware throughout the remainder of my flying years of the need to properly calculate the center of gravity for any mission involving cargo.

I was not the only one in Vietnam learning hard lessons. U.S. Army infantry units had begun to deploy to Vietnam in early 1965. Shortly after my slick mission, I was directed to respond to a 1st Infantry Division unit that had been ambushed close to their base. When I arrived, I landed and shut down my engine and went into the base camp to get a briefing. On the way in I noticed eight sets of boots and legs sticking out from under the side of a tent.

As the unit had done for several days in a row, they sent a squad to patrol around their position. Instead of working their way through the underbrush, the squad leader decided to take the easy route. He led his men down a trail directly into a Vietcong ambush. All of the Americans were killed and no enemy casualties were found. This was the precise point in the war when I came to realize that Americans soldiers were not supermen.

Those men lost their lives because they had a poor leader. Again and again during my years in Vietnam, I saw aircrews and ground troops killed and wounded because of faulty leadership. I had arrived in country with the mistaken idea that when our Army went into ground combat, it would do everything right, and would win the same way we had won in all of the war movies. Things just did not work out that way. In retrospect, I estimate that over half of the fifty thousand plus Americans killed in Vietnam were lost because of mistakes, over-aggressive leadership and accidents.

As mentioned earlier, we sometimes encountered targets that were too big or too dangerous for the light weapons systems on our aircraft. We quickly learned to back off and call for fighter-bomber support. In early 1965 there were no U.S. Air Force or Navy fighter-bombers in Vietnam. At this point in the war our politicians had not authorized them. However, there were South Vietnamese Air Force fighter-bombers and these units had U.S. Air Force advisors. Sometimes when we called for fighter-bomber support we found that one of the aircraft in the flight had an American advisor on board even though he had been specifically prohibited from flying in combat.

We called these pilots 'blue eyed Vietnamese Air Force' pilots, and it was a pleasure to be able to communicate clearly with them. When an American was aboard, the bombers would get in close and destroy the target. When we got a flight without an American, we had trouble talking to the pilots. They would usually drop their ordnance from high altitude and totally miss the target.

American fighter-bombers were finally introduced into combat in mid-February, 1965. The action that brought them in started on 7 February 1965 with an enemy sapper and mortar attack on Camp Holloway near Pleiku in the central highlands. Many Americans from the 119th Aviation Company were killed and wounded. Since most of their aircraft were damaged or destroyed in the attack, my platoon was sent to Pleiku the day after the attacks. We arrived to find smoke still rising from burnt out buildings and aircraft. I walked through the area and was amazed that the mortars had caused so much damage. There were holes in everything. From that point on, I had great respect for mortar fire.

While at Pleiku we were assigned a mission to provide overhead cover for a ground convoy of trucks bringing supplies and troops from the coastal town of Quy Nhon up to our location in the mountains. The convoy had to travel through the Mang Yang Pass where the Vietminh had successfully ambushed several French convoys in an earlier war. As a footnote, a famous French-Vietminh battle that took place in that Pass was the one depicted at the start of the 2002 Mel Gibson movie 'We Were Soldiers.'

The convoy cover mission was one that I had been training to accomplish since arriving in Vietnam. Generally, we would fly at about one thousand feet over the convoy. Since we flew about four or five times as fast at the convoy traveled, we were constantly flying over the vehicles from front to rear, then turning and flying from rear to front. The trick was to be in position and ready to fire at the first sign of an ambush. All of the vehicles had smoke grenades and at the first shot, the assistant drivers would throw their grenades on the side from which the fire was coming. We would immediately fire rockets and machine guns into the target area. Our suppressive fire would hopefully pin the enemy down long enough for the convoy to speed on by. This worked fine unless the enemy exploded a land mine under a vehicle and blocked the road.

Due to the great concern for the convoys that were going to travel through the Mang Yang Pass, General Westmoreland asked for and got approval to use U.S. Air Force and Navy fighter-bombers. We were excited to have the opportunity to be involved in the first true Joint Services mission of the war.

The American fighter pilots were much better than any I had seen before. In fact, they were almost too good. As the convoy traveled through the pass, the expected ambush took place. We fired our weapons but with little effect on the large number of enemy attackers. We called for air support and before we could look twice, the fighter-bombers came in on each side of us along the road and put their ordnance right on target. The bombs were so close that one of our door gunners received a wound from a friendly bomb fragment and we suffered holes in several of our aircraft. Thankfully, the convoy got through courtesy of the U.S. air support.

By May 1965 I had flown missions for most of the American advisory teams within a hundred mile radius of Saigon. These teams consisted of a small number of Americans that were stationed with Vietnamese forces. The bigger the supported unit, the more advisors it had assigned. At the basic lonely outpost you would find two or three advisors, while at a division headquarters you would find dozens. Their mission was the same at all locations: to coordinate the integration of U.S. assets into Vietnamese combat operations. This included advising them in their intelligence gathering and operational planning functions. These advisory teams were usually in isolated locations and were totally dependent on slick helicopters for their supplies, mail and transportation. Our armed helicopters supported them with frequent reconnaissance and fire support missions. We were also the first responders if they were attacked.

Routinely I received my orders for an advisory support mission the night before it was to be flown. I was told when and where to report, and how much 'blade time' I was to give them. Blade time was our term for the number of flying hours I was authorized to fly in support of the unit. Once I flew that amount of time, I was through for the day and could come home (unless there was an emergency).

Upon arrival at the mission site, I would be briefed on what the advisory team wanted us to accomplish. This could include area or route reconnaissance, support of a ground operation, target attack and about anything they could dream up. Usually, the American advisor would ride along in my helicopter, and his Vietnamese counterpart would ride with my wingman.

We would usually fly several ninety minute missions during the day. After each we would return to the airfield to rearm and refuel. Often the crews would find bullet holes as they performed visual inspections of the aircraft before taking off again. The crew chief would carefully examine the area between the entry and exit holes to make sure no vital component had been hit. If there was serious damage we would call our unit. They would send a maintenance team with parts to fix the problem. If the problem was not serious, we would apply duct tape over the holes. We called it 'hundred miles an hour tape' because it would strip off if we exceeded that speed. We used lots of duct tape.

Crew chief uses duct tape to temporarily repair bullet holes. Note that the ground is completely covered with empty machine gun cartridges.

One day in late May, when I reported for a mission, the advisor seemed amazed that I was there. He soon told me that the word was out that I had been killed. This went on for two or three days at different places. I was puzzled until I found out that a Lieutenant (Philip) Childers, who I did not know, had in fact been killed on 28 May 1965. He had been flying a UH-1 'slick' from the 118th Assault Helicopter Company, and was involved in a mid-air collision with another helicopter. Both crews were killed. Eyes were raised several times over the next month whenever I showed up alive to support different advisory teams. This was not the kind of notoriety I enjoyed.

On 12 June 1965 Chief Warrant Officer Billy Hammer was killed. He was the second loss among the four of us who had volunteered for the UTT. Billy had been reassigned out of our unit and sent to a newly arriving unit, Company A of the 82nd Aviation Battalion. It was standard procedure at that time to send each new unit a few experienced pilots, and he got caught up in this rotation. Billy was flying a night mission with Warrant Officer Mike Wildes when their helicopter ran into low clouds and bad weather. Hammer was a small man and had a lot of flying experience. Wildes was a larger man, and had little flying experience. Their size and experience differences were determined to be contributors to their death.

They were flying on instruments (no visual reference to the ground), inside a cloud in total darkness. They had good communications with the control tower at our airfield. All was going well until an argument erupted in the cockpit, which was monitored on the radio by the control tower. One of the pilots (thought to be Wildes), had become disoriented with vertigo, thinking the helicopter was upside down. They began to fight over the controls, causing the aircraft to roll upside down and crash killing all four crewmembers. The crash site was discovered the next morning when the weather cleared. The helicopter had hit the ground in an upright attitude with a high rate of descent, and burned. The dead crew was still strapped into their seats.

This incident caused all of us to gain a new appreciation for the importance of constantly being prepared for emergency instrument flying and renewed our efforts to practice it in good weather. We did so by having one of the pilots in each aircraft fly with a 'hood' over his eyes so he could see only the instruments. The other pilot served as the safety, keeping an eye out for other aircraft.

As I mentioned earlier, new helicopter pilots coming out of flight school at the time I graduated received only marginal instrument flight training. As a result, there were a lot of accidents like the one described above. The Army finally fixed the problem in 1966 when it extended initial flight training a few weeks to include qualification for an instrument ticket (competent to make preplanned flights in clouds). Shortly after completing my tour in Vietnam I was sent back to Fort Rucker to complete training for an instrument ticket.

Only a week after Hammer was killed, I found out that my flight school class leader, Captain Roberto Samaniego had been killed. Assigned to the 119th Assault Helicopter Company in the central highlands of Vietnam as a slick pilot, he was performing an emergency ammunition supply mission into an outpost that was under attack. On short final approach the aircraft was hit by ground fire, caught fire, and exploded, killing all aboard. I was saddened by the news and again glad that I was not flying slicks.

The UH-1 air assault helicopter companies then in Vietnam were organized into two platoons of slick helicopters and one platoon of gunships. Their gunships were essentially like ours but their primary mission was to escort the troop carrying slicks. During large scale air assaults involving several companies there was a need for helicopters that were not involved in escorting slicks to make an initial reconnaissance of the landing area, neutralize any enemy found, mark exact landing spots with smoke grenades and recommend routes into and out of the area. This duty fell to our company, and was a huge responsibility upon which the success of the entire operation depended.

By June 1965, I was usually selected by my leaders to perform the reconnaissance portion of this task. The company commander or platoon leader would be in overall command and I made my recommendations to him. He would then relay the information to the task force commander, who would ultimately make the decisions. Maybe I was lucky, but we never lost a troop carrying aircraft in any of the assaults that I worked.

An example of one of these missions gone wrong took place on 9 February 1965, near the end of the battle at Binh Gia. Our Raider Platoon, commanded by Captain Jack Johnson, was supporting an airlift of Vietnamese troops. During the operation the enemy troops held fire and were not detected during the reconnaissance. As the slick helicopters landed the Vietcong opened fire and shot down two of them. Both crashed and burned.

One of our guns ships escorting slicks was shot down, killing the copilot and wounding the crew chief. Later in the day we lost another aircraft that was providing overhead cover for the ground troops. This crew was wounded but successfully evacuated. Two more pilots were wounded that day including Captain Johnson. I had been supporting the battle, but was away refueling and rearming when the losses occurred. My luck was holding!

In about May 1965 I was notified that I would participate in a top secret mission involving the first attempt to use helicopters dropping tear gas to force the enemy from hiding places. The high command had great concern that the news media would find out about what we were planning and report it as the introduction of chemical warfare in Vietnam. In reality, tear gas was accepted world-wide as a 'crowd control' compound and was not related to deadly chemical agents. We were told that we could not even talk to each other about what was being planned.

A simple modification was made to our 2.75 inch rocket pods to allow us to drop hundreds of tear gas hand grenades at once. We carried one pod on each side of the aircraft and each pod contained seven tubes. The front end of each tube was blocked and a spring was inserted from the rear. Next, about a dozen grenades were inserted, with safety pins pulled, into the tube. As each was inserted the spring was put under more and more pressure. Finally, the rear was blocked with a pin that could be pulled by the door gunner using a wire lanyard.

For our mission the entire crew was issued gas masks. Since they were full face masks, they interfered with our ability to see and to talk on the radio. Therefore, only half of the crew would wear the masks at one time unless gas somehow got inside the aircraft. As I recall, there were five aircraft involved, two to drop gas, two to attack any enemy that emerged from the targeted area, and a command and control aircraft. My fire team was the attack team.

While we were preparing for takeoff our Company Commander Major Jaggers, who was flying the command and control aircraft, came on the radio and asked: "Aaaa, this is Saber Six, how do you hear me through my gas mask"? We almost fell out of our aircraft laughing because the boss had just transmitted to the world what we had been told to not even mention. No harm was done and Jim had put another notch in his reputation for saying what was on his mind.

We flew a few miles south of Saigon to a suspected enemy bunker complex that was under a tree line and along a canal. The gas carrying aircraft swooped down and dropped their grenades. An area about fifty feet wide by two hundred feet long was immediately saturated with the white smoke of about two hundred grenades. I circled at an altitude of several hundred feet watching and waiting for the gas to work its magic. I expected dozens of enemy soldiers to stagger into the open but nothing happened. Nothing!

I made a high reconnaissance then escorted the commander on a low pass to try to draw enemy fire and get a closer look, but still we heard nothing and saw nothing. Finally, in frustration, we backed off and expended our rockets and machine guns on the target area. We flew back in for a post-strike reconnaissance but saw no evidence that the enemy had ever been there. I do not know how this mission was reported up the chain of command, but it must have been considered unsuccessful because we never got another gas mission. I have always been curious about how the war might have changed if someone had selected a better target for that test.

Of all the bad things that can happen on board an armed helicopter, the most feared is a fire. Loaded with ammunition and fuel, a fire could easily destroy a critical component before the crew could get the aircraft on the ground. Therefore, any time we heard a radio transmission indication someone had a fire on board their aircraft, we held our breath.

Just before Jim Jaggers completed his tour of duty with our company in June 1965, he commanded a large air assault mission several miles northwest of Saigon. It was a night mission which always heightened our concerns. The simplest problem with any of the helicopters involved in a night assault could result in disaster. In addition, a downed aircraft at night would take focus and priority away from accomplishing the assault mission and put it on recovering the downed crew.

As the troop carriers approached their landing area on this particular mission, Jim came on the primary command radio and said in his slow talking, easily recognizable voice: "Aaaa, this is Saber 6, stand by one, I am on fire." In about a hundred cockpits, several hundred of us simultaneously had the same question: how could anyone sound so calm with such an impending disaster? Most of us would have been screaming on the radio for help but not Jim. In a few minutes he came back on the air to tell us that his crew had successfully extinguished the fire. Through his calm approach, he had put us at ease and contributed to the ultimate success of the mission. This incident was a crowning moment in Jim's outstanding tour as our commander

Sometime in June 1965 Major Pete Booth assumed command of the company. A tall, quiet, and very smart officer, Pete had some big shoes to fill. As in any military change of command, the new person is looked upon with some skepticism until he proves himself. This is especially true in a combat environment. Major Booth, aware of this, elected to learn from the bottom up by flying with some of the experienced fire teams before attempting to lead his own.

I was directed to help train Major Booth on the techniques for conducting reconnaissance missions. By that time in my tour I had developed reconnaissance techniques to a high degree. Using the Cardinal Rules, I had learned how to effectively use the terrain, enemy situation, wind and sun in minimizing risk while maximizing results on these missions.

The reconnaissance mission was normally initiated when I received map coordinates and available enemy intelligence regarding the target. I would study the map to select an approach route, and arrive in the area at an altitude of about twelve hundred feet. I would fly a high reconnaissance first, selectively and incrementally exposing my aircraft, hoping to draw fire. I almost never saw the enemy from this altitude.

If no fire was forthcoming I would initiate the transition to low level flight. I would back away from the target and use the best combination of jungle cover, sun and wind to mask my descent through the 'dead man zone.' I would plan to end up over the target while in a turn, flying downwind with the sun behind me. Obviously, all of these conditions could not always be achieved. It was up to me to maximize those that I could.

If enemy forces were present, they usually shot at me as I appeared over the target. If I had performed my job correctly, the enemy would fail to lead my aircraft properly and not get a hit. My wingman, covering me from behind, would dump a load of rockets and we would both retreat and gain altitude. I would then either line up and make several gun runs, call in artillery or put in a flight of fighters, depending on which was available or appropriate.

I flew several of these missions with Major Booth. He must have liked my technique because he selected me to give some reconnaissance training to the gun platoon leader of a new assault helicopter company that had recently arrived. This turned out to be a pleasant experience for me because the individual that showed up to be trained was the same individual that had refused to accept me in his armed helicopter platoon at Fort Benning. I was tempted to remind him that I was ROTC, but both of us recognized the irony of the situation, and never mentioned his rejection. I hope he made it home alive.

In June 1965 our platoon leader, Captain Dick Jarrett, was replaced by another 'new guy,' Captain Bill Fraker. The new Playboy 'Daddy Rabbit' (as the Playboy platoon leader was called), had another set of big shoes to fill. It was hard to see Dick go because we trusted and respected him with the loyalty that can only be generated in extreme situations like combat. He was dedicated to getting the job done without unduly risking our lives, and we appreciated that.

If I had to characterize Dick in one word, it would be 'serious.' He was especially serious about operating according to the Cardinal Rules. This could in part be attributed to the fact that while flying on one of his first combat missions, on 12 August 1964 his copilot, First Lieutenant Harold McNeil, was killed instantly when a round came through his windshield and hit him in the chest. McNeil was flying the aircraft and trying to stay in position to cover the fire team leader, who for some reason ignored the Cardinal Rules and flew down the center of a clearing directly into the enemy positions. Dick was barely able to grab the controls in time to save the aircraft from crashing.

Captain Fraker came in as an unknown quantity. He was new in country and like all new guys, needed to prove he could function in combat before being fully accepted. Some guys were good and some were lucky. I would characterize Bill as being was both. He had early success on night missions and started building a reputation as cavalier and fearless. This typified the remainder of his tour. In June 1965 he was awarded a Distinguished Service Cross, the second highest combat award, for flying into an enemy held compound under withering enemy fire and rescuing some American advisors. General Westmoreland had observed the action and ordered the award on the spot.

Later, as he prepared for reassignment as the company operation officer, Bill started training his replacement, Captain Don Clark. On 11 September 1965, during one of his first missions, Don was killed. Bill had ordered him to take it easy until he learned the ropes. However, Don ignored the order and tried a high risk maneuver. He was hovering at night down a canal below the treetops looking for enemy boats with his searchlight. He had violated several of the Cardinal Rules and enemy fire shot out his tail rotor, causing the aircraft to crash. Fortunately, the other three members of the crew survived and were rescued by the wingman.

At this point in my tour I was really up tight. I asked for and was granted ten days of leave. The military had not yet started scheduled rest and recuperation (R&R), so I had to make my own way to wherever I wanted to go. I called Mary Jane and asked her to meet me in Honolulu. She was having a rough time keeping up with out two babies, so she needed no encouragement. Her parents were kind enough to keep the children. She flew to Hawaii, getting there before I did. I finally arrived on a 'space available' flight and we had a joyous reunion and our first real honeymoon.

On the third night in Honolulu we wandered into a nightclub that advertised a local singer and band. There was no cover charge but we had to buy at least two drinks. We thoroughly enjoyed the show, later known as the Don Ho Show. His music was so good that we went back the next night and stayed for the whole show again. We had no idea that Don Ho would become a superstar. We still enjoy his songs forty years later.

CHAPTER 7

THE WAR GETS TOUGH

Our toughest missions involved medical evacuation of wounded soldiers. The presence of wounded was a pretty good guarantee that the enemy was in the area. They seemed to know when we had casualties. They would try to ambush any aircraft that approached the area by guessing our approach path and setting up machine guns along it. As I gained experience, I was able to anticipate the enemy most of the time. From the air I could see the complete layout of the terrain and had my choice of approach routes. Usually, I would come in over the heaviest jungle available.

When time permitted, we would call for special medical evacuation helicopters to actually land and perform the pickup while we provided escort and covering fire. This was preferred because our gunships were fully loaded down with weapons and ammunition and we had a hard time lifting off with the extra weight of wounded soldiers. Also, the medical evacuation helicopters had a medic on board who could administer blood and other assistance on the way to the hospital. These special helicopters had the radio call sign 'Dustoff,' and since they risked their life to save others on almost every mission, they were the most respected helicopter crews in Vietnam.

When I was called to escort Dustoff I would try to arrive over the battle area first. It was my job to locate the friendly forces and find out where the enemy was located so I could route Dustoff around and away from them. Simply stated, I was trolling for ground fire, asking to be shot at. Of course, I tried to be as smart as possible and use all of the Cardinal Rules to my advantage. If fire was received, I would suppress it with rockets and machine guns and fall in behind Dustoff on his final approach to landing. Taking into account the location of the friendly forces, I would fire on either side of him as he landed, circle around while continuing to fire to keep the enemy's head down, then fly and fire beside him as he took off. This was called 'shooting him in and out of the landing zone.'

On my first medical evacuation mission in January 1965, I was not as smart as I would become later. I was flying a reconnaissance mission north of Saigon when I got a report that one South Vietnamese soldier and one American advisor had been badly wounded and needed evacuation immediately if they were to live. This was still early in the war and American casualties on the ground were rare. We would do almost anything to help save an American life.

Since there was no time to wait for a Dustoff aircraft, I decided to land and pick up the wounded and fly them to the hospital. The ground troops threw a smoke grenade and I could tell that there was about twenty mph of wind. My wingman gave me good covering fire and I approached to land, flying directly into the wind as we had been taught in flight school. In my haste I had ignored the Cardinal Rules.

Before starting the approach I was flying at about ninety mph. With the headwind my ground speed was really slow. Not smart! On our first pass we received heavy ground fire and took some hits in and around the cockpit. None of us were wounded so I circled and made the approach and landing from another direction.

I knew we were too heavy to get back into the air with the added weight of the wounded, so I had the door gunners toss out onto the ground most of their door gun ammunition. As I considered my options for a take off path the dream I described earlier came to mind: 'go with the wind.' I got airborne into the wind but as soon as I was above the tree tops I turned downwind.

With the tail wind my ground speed was now about one hundred and ten mph. This took me back near the enemy positions but because of the added forty mph of ground speed, the ground fire was well behind me and I only took a couple of rounds in the tail boom. The mission had been a total success except for all of the bullet holes that had to be patched that night.

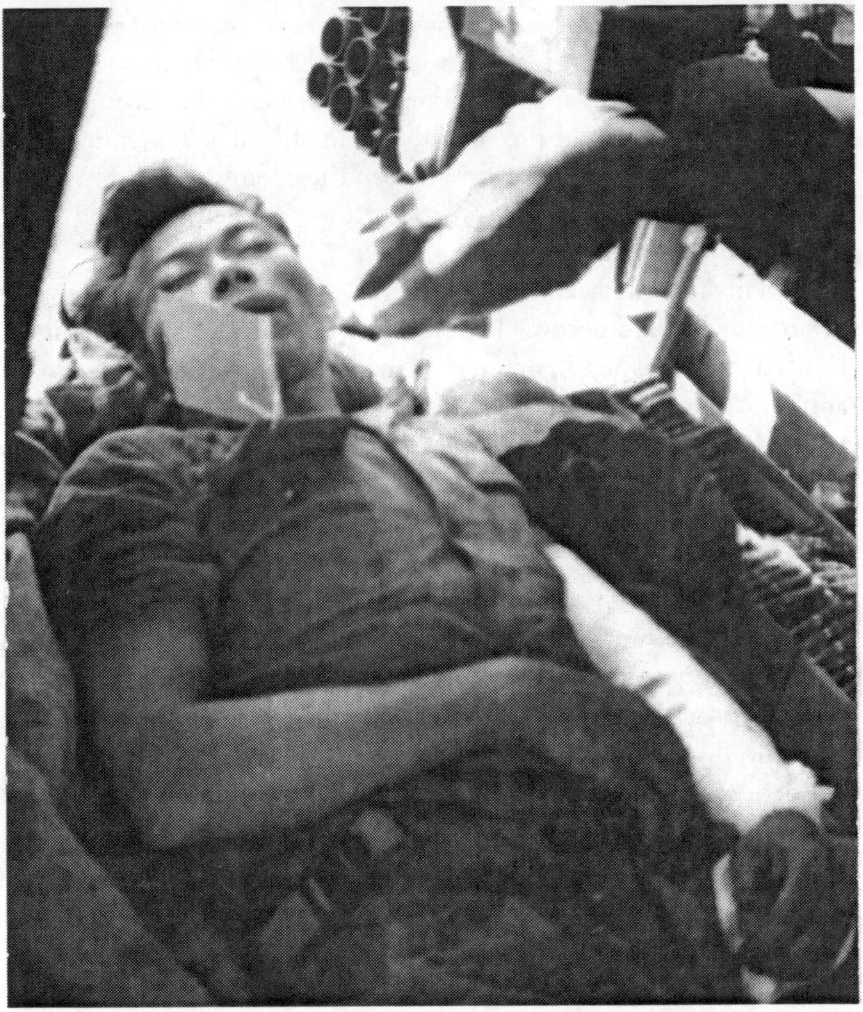

A wounded and tagged Vietnamese soldier being evacuated. With all the weapons and ammunition in the aircraft there was not much room for carrying wounded, but we often did it.

In about July 1965, I was introduced to a mission I flew often in the next few months. It was in support of Air Force C-123 cargo aircraft spraying Agent Orange Defoliant on the Jungle. The C-123 is a two engine aircraft of Korean War vintage that had been rigged with a tank inside and a set of spray tubes across the back. At its slowest speed it flew about twenty mph faster than our helicopters.

C-123s like this one with combat damage were used to spray the Agent Orange defoliant in Vietnam.

Because of the speed differential, I had to lead my fire team in ahead of their flight. We would approach the drop zone with one helicopter on each side of the spray aircraft's intended flight path and start shooting. The C-123s would then dive down between us, turn on their spray and eventually fly past us before completing their run. As you might imagine, these big lumbering aircraft were a favorite target of the Vietcong.

Before each mission I would meet with the Air Force Pilots to coordinate operational details. I was always surprised to see that their aircraft were literally covered with bullet holes. Unlike the Army who tried to camouflage our bullet holes, the C-123 crews painted each patch orange. They truly looked like polka-dotted aircraft.

For some reason, I was careful not to fly through the spray as it came out of the aircraft, and to my knowledge was never exposed to Agent Orange. I do remember the smell of it because I walked around and inside several of the spray aircraft as they were being loaded. By being cautious I had unknowingly protected my fire team from the horrible effects of Agent Orange that became known only at a much later date.

Sometime in August I was launched on an emergency mission to find two fuel tanker trucks that had been stolen by the Vietcong. The report said they were headed up a dirt road north of Saigon that led into the jungle in an area known as War Zone D. There were several war zones around that part of the country. They were occupied by the enemy, and were called free fire zones. We had clearance to fire at anything we found in one of these zones. More about that later.

After about thirty minutes of flying up the road we located the trucks parked under a huge monkey pod tree. They looked just like any fuel truck you would see on the interstate highway in America. The Vietcong were busy trying to cover them with cut tree branches. When they saw us, they scrambled away into the jungle. I called headquarters on the radio and asked for instructions. Since the sun was about to set it was decided that a ground assault could not be launched in time to prevent the enemy from moving and hiding the trucks during the night.

I was ordered to destroy the trucks. We seldom had such a juicy target so this came as a welcome surprise. I first made a normal gun run with rockets from about one thousand feet but they exploded in the tree tops. I decided I would have to go down low and get the rockets under the trees. However, my wingman Jim Lee had a better idea. He suggested we get in close enough to fire machine guns into the trucks. If you get within a few hundred feet of a target, machine gun tracer rounds are still burning when they hit. Since every fifth round in a belt of machine gun ammunition is a tracer, almost any target would burn when hit with a burst at close range.

After a careful high reconnaissance, I backed off about a mile and got down on the deck. I took one truck and my wingman the other. We fired at about the same time and both trucks were hit simultaneously. Just like in the movies, there was a tremendous fireball rolling up in front of me. I banked away just in time to avoid flying into it. I circled the area a few times and just watched the expanding fire. This was to be the second most memorable firing pass I would ever make. The most memorable one was to occur in 1968 while flying an AH-1 Cobra on my second combat tour.

During my youth I had seen many movies and news clips showing U.S. Air Force fighters diving down strafing railroads and truck convoys. Only once during my combat flying did I get the opportunity to make a similar attack. In keeping with the nature of the Vietnam War, my convoy was not trucks and tanks, but supply wagons being pulled by water buffaloes.

This action came shortly after I destroyed the tanker trucks. A Vietcong unit had overrun a friendly village during the night and was trying to escape back into the jungle before it got light enough for the inevitable helicopters came. Unfortunately for them, their timing was bad. My fire team had been launched before dawn to assist the village. I arrived to find a few survivors and a flaming arrow pointing up a road to the north. It was standard practice at that time for all Vietnamese outposts to have an arrow about ten feet long formed from several firepots (cans filled with sand and fuel) mounted on a swivel inside the compound. When attacked, the firepots were lit and the arrow pointed toward the enemy so responding aircraft would know where to look and fire.

As dawn approached I flew north at about one thousand feet looking for any activity or ground fire. Suddenly I saw what looked like a group of farmers on about seven oxcarts headed up the road. I make a high pass trying to get a good look and expecting to get shot at if it was the enemy. I have to give them credit for good discipline because they held their fire. Not satisfied with what I saw, I backed off and descended below the top of the trees and came in fast about ten feet over their heads. As I popped into sight, several of the carts threw off tarps exposing twenty to thirty armed men. They started to shoot at me, but because of my high speed and low altitude downwind approach, I was there and gone so fast that neither of my aircraft was hit.

The convoy was on a trail that passed through some ride paddies that were a few hundred yards from thick jungle. For some reason, the Vietcong decided not to scatter, which would have complicated my problem. I flew out about a half mile and climbed to twelve hundred feet, turned in, lined up and entered a shallow dive. When I got into range I let go with rockets and machine guns. It was just like the movies. There were enemy soldiers diving out in all directions, and a couple of carts exploded as I hit some of their ammunition. I circled and concentrated my fire on the scattering troops and did not fire any more at the carts. For some reason, I had no stomach for killing the defenseless water buffaloes. I stayed until our ammunition was expended and departed, having achieved a small victory and engraved an unforgettable moment on my brain.

This was not my last encounter with animals. During a low altitude reconnaissance of a jungle area north of Song Be I spotted four elephants. They had some boxes strapped onto their backs and were in a free fire zone, so they were pretty clearly transporting Vietcong equipment. I called the ground sector commander on the radio and reported what I had seen. He told me: "wait while I look at the signal operating instructions to see what that code word means." I told him it was not a code word. I had seen real elephants. It took a while to convince him that I had found the real thing.

I asked what he wanted me to do about them. I did not want to shoot them unless I was sure that they were carrying enemy equipment, and that I had a clearance to do so. He instructed me: "try to draw ground fire, and if the enemy defends the elephants, destroy everything." I flew high, then low and slow over the area several times with no luck. The sector commander decided to put some forces on the ground to check them out. I gave him a good fix on their location and departed to refuel. While that was taking place my team was diverted to another mission. I never did find out what happened to the elephants.

It was not unusual to spot groups of wild pigs running around in the jungle. We knew that the Vietcong used them as a primary source of food. Therefore we were instructed to destroy them anytime they were found in free fire zones. I would normally assign a door gunner this task because it was good target practice.

The door gunners of Gene Fudge's fire team shot a huge pig near an open area in the jungle. Gene was able to land and his crew loaded it into the helicopter and delivered it to the company cook. I heard that the enlisted men had a great feast the next day. I never did find out what a wild Vietnamese pig tasted like.

I did, however, find out what cooked dog tastes like. While supporting Vietnamese units we usually landed at lunch time and ate with them. We would eat our C rations and they would eat their food, usually rice and fish, pork or chicken. One day we were offered some grilled meat that had been cooked on small wooden sticks. It looked and smelled pretty good so we accepted. After the meal, the American advisor with the Vietnamese unit told us we had just eaten dog meat. I flew the rest of the day with a little knot in my stomach. From then on, I always asked about the food before I ate it.

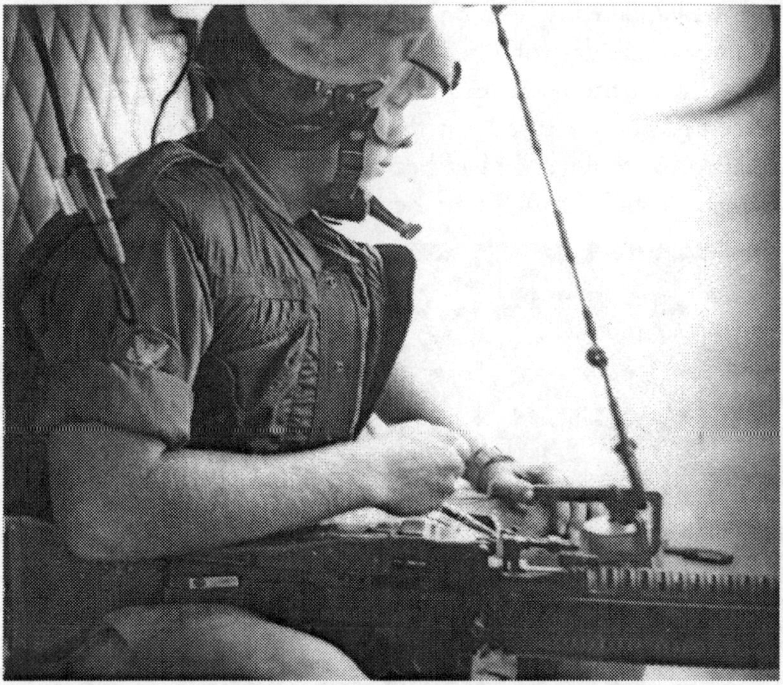

Door gunner ready for action with flack jacket on and helmet visor down. His M-60 machine gun is supported by a rubber cord.

This was not the last time I was to eat strange food. On a trip to Hong Kong that I will discuss later, I purchased a stereo for a Vietnamese couple that worked for our company. They paid for the stereo and invited me to dinner at a Vietnamese restaurant to say thanks. The first course of the meal was some kind of soup. It looked like a beef broth with some items floating around in it, and was served in a big bowl in the center of the table. We dipped our own servings. I reluctantly dished out only liquid and it tasted salty and pretty good. When we got near the bottom of the bowl, I saw an eyeball floating there. As it turned out we were eating bird soup. My friends told me that it was tradition to save the eyeball for the guest of honor, meaning me. Thankfully, it was small and I was able to swallow it without chewing. This was the last time I ever accepted an invitation to a traditional Vietnamese meal.

In late August my friend Carl Mangold and I started to plan a five day trip to Singapore. By that time in the war the Army had started to give each soldier one five day leave during a tour. I didn't remind anyone that I had already been on a ten day leave so the trip was approved with a departure date of 2 September 1965.

Carl was a fire team leader in the Raider Platoon. He frequently asserted in a good natured way that his fire team was better than mine. I returned the dialog. We had become friends in flight school and followed each other through Fort Benning and into our current jobs.

Carl Mangold (left) and I relax in our lounge and compare notes on the day's action shortly before he and his crew were killed in action.

On the first of September, the day before our planned departure, we were both assigned one last mission. Carl's fire team was to remain on call at the airfield on 'standby' to respond immediately to emergency situations, and my mission was to escort a ground convoy that was traveling on a dangerous road north from Saigon.

Part of our preparations for the leave was for one of us to go into downtown Saigon to exchange our American dollars for Singapore dollars. Since I knew where the exchange station was located, we decided that I should have that task. There was one problem. My convoy escort mission could last until dark. I might not get back in time to exchange the money. Carl's standby mission ended at 5:00 PM, well before the exchange station closed. Therefore, we simply traded missions. This seemingly small decision turned out to be one that ended or changed the lives of many.

At about 1:00 PM on 1 September 1965, while flying at about one thousand feet above the convoy, Carl's helicopter exploded and crashed. All on board were instantly killed. As the emergency standby fire team, I was immediately launched to the area. All I was told initially was that an aircraft was down. En route I was briefed on the radio that it was Carl's aircraft, and that there were no survivors. I was stunned and numb.

Upon arrival in the area I flew low over the smoking crash site. All I could see was a black hole and some pieces of rotor blades. Slick helicopters were arriving to recover the remains. I was ordered to sweep the area for enemy positions and provide overhead security for the recovery operation. I began a low altitude sweep around the area. I really, really wanted to find something to shoot. I flew with my skids in the trees until my fuel was almost gone, but saw nothing suspicious. I returned to the airfield with a heavy heart. Obviously, there would be no trip the next day.

At that time it was assumed that Carl's aircraft had been downed by enemy fire. Eyewitnesses on the ground, and Carl's wingman reported that they observed a big explosion near the aircraft. Over the years, I have heard several different theories on the source of that explosion, all unproven. The first and most probable one was that enemy gunfire hit one of his rocket pods and caused it to explode. Another was that an enemy shoulder fired rocket propelled grenade (RPG) had hit the aircraft. The RPG was designed for use against vehicles and bunkers. A few had been fired at helicopters in Vietnam, most unsuccessful. They have been much more successful in recent years in Iraq, Afghanistan and Somalia.

A third theory was that the Vietnamese observer onboard was in fact a Vietcong, and had pulled the pin on a hand grenade to commit suicide and destroy the aircraft. A final theory was that Carl had unknowingly flown through the gun target line of a Vietnamese 105 millimeter field artillery battery. Reportedly, investigation showed that the artillery was firing rounds with proximity fuses in Carl's direction at the time of the explosion. A proximity fuse uses radar to detonate the round just before it hits the target. Like all of the other theories, this would explain the reports of an explosion near the aircraft. Unfortunately, the real truth will never be known. Carl was the third loss among the group of four that volunteered for the UTT back in 1964. I could not help but wonder if I was next.

Four days after the loss of Carl and his crew, the Playboys lost Warrant Officer John LaGrand. John was a relatively new guy in our platoon. He had a friend who was a U.S. Air Force pilot. The pilot was serving as an advisor to the Vietnamese Air Force, and had invited John to fly as his copilot in an A1-E Sky Raider fighter-bomber. While on this flight the aircraft was seen to dive into the jungle and explode, killing both of them. Following this incident, we received orders that restricted us to flying only assigned missions in assigned aircraft. We were losing enough pilots without losing more needlessly.

I violated the order to stay out of other unit's aircraft only once. Some days after LaGrand went in we were supporting an operation in the 'horseshoe' area of the Dong Nai River west of Saigon. During a medical evacuation mission a Dustoff crew had accidentally left a medic on the ground. The aircraft had landed to pick up some wounded Vietnamese and the medics jumped out to assist in loading. All of a sudden, the enemy opened up on the aircraft. The pilot, not knowing one of the medics was still outside the aircraft, took off. He circled around and tried to get back to the medic but the aircraft was badly shot up and could not land.

An air assault was quickly put together to try to rescue the missing medic. My fire team was pulled off of another mission and sent to perform the landing zone reconnaissance. In preparation I landed near several airlift aircraft on a friendly airstrip a few miles from the objective area. I was invited to join the mission commander aboard a 'slick' that was going to climb to a high altitude and fly over the 'horseshoe' to make an on-the-scene plan of action. I got caught up in the frantic nature of the mission and found myself in the crew compartment of the slick, feet hanging out the door, an automatic rifle in my hands and no seat belt.

As we climbed to altitude I realized how foolish this was, and how it violated every thing I knew about flight safety. The reconnaissance was uneventful and I was extremely happy when I got back on the ground and safely strapped into the seat of my own aircraft. I held my breath for a few days in fear that my boss, Captain Fraker, would find out about my disregard for his orders, but nothing was ever said.

In spite of a huge operation that we launched, the medic was never found, nor was his body recovered. For months we heard rumors that he was taken prisoner, but to my knowledge, he was not returned at the end of the war.

Eight days after Carl's death, on 9 September, I was promoted to Captain. The ceremony was conducted on a remote airstrip in the middle of a combat operation. Upon landing to refuel and rearm, I was met by my Company Commander, Major Booth, and told to report to Lieutenant Colonel Chuck Honour who was waiting in the refueling area. Chuck was the Commander of the 145th Aviation Battalion, to which our company was assigned. I figured that I had done something bad.

Upon reporting to him I was surprised when he pinned Captain's bars on me. Sadly, Chuck, his entire crew and several passengers were killed on 18 February 1966 when he flew into a wire near Bien Hoa. The wire he hit was near the one that had taken the life of my friend Lyal Erwin about a year earlier.

On 9 September 1965 Lt. Colonel Chuck Honour pinned on my new Captains bars as Major Pete Booth looks on. Chuck was later killed.

My promotion to Captain was both bitter and sweet for me. One day I was one of a few highly experienced Lieutenant fire team leaders in the country. I had been selected to help train our Commander, Major Booth, when he arrived. I had also trained platoon leaders for newly arriving units. I had a good combat record and my recommendations regarding combat operations were taken seriously. However, when I was promoted, I was just another of many Captains who seemed to be everywhere. If it had not been for the pay raise, I would have preferred to complete my tour with the rank of Lieutenant.

Not all of our casualties were people. Sometimes we lost a beloved helicopter. One that comes to mind was Dick Jarrett's 'Hog,' which was our name for the platoon leader's special aircraft. It was equipped to carry forty eight rockets instead of the fourteen that the fire team aircraft normally carried. Thus, it was much heavier than ours, and required more pilot skills to take off and land. Dick was proud of his Hog. He had the systems tuned to his particular way of flying and shooting and would seldom let anyone else fly it. On one occasion he

Captain Dick Jarrett the Playboy Platoon Leader with his aircraft tail number 944. It was armed with 'Hog pods' that carried forty eight rockets.

Dick Jarrett reluctantly took a day off and Gene Fudge, another Playboy fire team leader, killed Dick's 'Hog' when he crashed it near the village of Phouc Vinh.

took a needed day off and reluctantly turned his pride and joy over to the other Captain in the platoon, Gene Fudge. Gene was assigned to support my fire team on a reconnaissance mission around Phouc Vinh. We landed at the airfield to get a briefing and refuel. As we headed out to begin our mission Gene led our takeoff. He cleared the runway and was over a village when I observed that his rotor blades were slowing down. The aircraft slowly lost altitude and crashed into a group of houses. The helicopter was destroyed but luckily there was no fire and the crew walked away. The exact cause of the crash was never determined but Gene got the blame. That day became known as the 'day that Fudge killed Jarrett's Hog.' Dick was issued another hog and to my knowledge, nobody but him flew that one until after he completed his tour with the platoon.

Combat losses were piling up all around me. I was starting to feel the pressure. I needed a break so I applied for a five day leave to Hong Kong. I justified it as a make up for the one I had not used earlier. It was approved quickly. This time I did not plan to go with anybody else!

Upon arrival, a Chinese tailor shop owner was there to meet me. He had been hosting members of the UTT for years. His underlying motivation was to sell suits and uniforms but he also served as a tour guide.

The first place he took me was to his shop to measure me and write my clothing order. I contracted for a civilian suit, mess blue and white Army uniforms, and several other items. The prices were unbelievably low. Some of the uniforms lasted for twenty five years and when I retired, I gave them to my son Bill, an Army Captain at that time. With some minor modifications, he was able to continue to use them for years.

After being measured I was taken to the Peninsula hotel, which was considered to be the finest in Hong Kong. The first thing I wanted was fresh milk. There was no fresh milk in Vietnam at the time, and it had been months since I had tasted it. Next I ordered an American style corned beef sandwich. Milk and corned beef became my main food over the remainder of the stay. Between fittings for my new clothes I was toured around to see the sights, and was treated to some great Chinese food. The stay was over in the blink of an eye, but it had re-charged my batteries and I was ready to go back and finish up my tour in Vietnam.

This is how my Warrant Officers said I kept them in line. Acting the part here outside our villa is Warrant Officer 'Breeze' Elmore.

We logged a lot of time on five minute alert at the airstrip. Here my copilot Kent Paxton (right) and our gunner and crew chief grab some needed rest.

CHAPTER 8

TESTING NEW WEAPONS

Sometime in mid-1964 I was notified that my fire team had been selected to participate in another classified mission. The high command had decided to test the use of B-52 bombers dropping large numbers of bombs on enemy bunker and tunnel complexes.

The plan was simple: A radio beacon would be set up at a friendly location a few miles from the target. The B-52s (they flew in flights of two), would home in on the beacon, and upon crossing it, turn to the heading that would take them outbound over the target. Since these targets were in the jungle and invisible from the air, the B-52s would fly a calculated amount time outbound from the beacon, then drop their bombs. Computers were used to calculate minor changes to the course, speed and time to account for variables such as wind direction and speed.

The target for this first mission was a tunnel complex that reportedly held an enemy supply depot. It was located about fifty miles northeast of Saigon. The beacon was set up on an airfield at the village of Phouc Vinh, about ten miles east of the target. My mission was to orbit my fire team just outside the target area until the bombs landed, then swoop in low level just as the dust cleared to do a post strike assessment. I had some observers on board who would take photos and help judge the success of the bombing mission.

It was a clear, sunny day. I did not know the altitude of the approaching two B-52s, but they flew so high that we could barely see them. I received a countdown to impact on the radio and turned toward the target in time to see a couple of hundred seven hundred and fifty pound bombs hit the jungle in two long, closely spaced lines. The world absolutely exploded in front of me.

I descended to tree top level, accelerated to maximum speed (about one hundred and twenty mph), and zoomed over the devastated area. There in front of me were huge holes in the jungle, each about the size of a tennis court. They were strung together like beads in a chain. In the first few holes I saw only dirt and splintered trees. However as I progressed down the line I began to pick up obvious man-made items. Most were unidentifiable, but they were generally blue, white and brown. As I approached the center of the strike area I observed literally thousands of these items. I was busy flying the aircraft and trying to stay in the best position for the observers to view the scene, so could not focus on the items in the craters.

They were later identified as uniforms, weapons and hospital supplies that had been inside the targeted tunnels, and what was left of the enemy soldiers who had the misfortune to be working there. As ordered, I completed this one pass and did not return because of concern for our safety. Later in the war it was standard practice for helicopters to go in and hover around in the bomb craters to pick up items that might be of use to the intelligence community.

This first B-52 bombing mission was judged to be an overwhelming success. From that day forward, their strikes became business as usual in the war. I observed dozens of them as the fighting intensified on this and future tours.

As I indicated earlier, our Huey Helicopter was designed in the late 1950s as a medical evacuation machine, and was never intended to carry guns. Also, the concept of employing helicopters in low intensity warfare was new. In 1965 the U.S. military-industrial complex was madly scrambling to develop equipment to improve our machine's effectiveness and survivability. At the same time the Army Aviation School was trying to document our tactics so they could train the increasing number of new pilots they were producing.

Our unit had pioneered most of the armed helicopter tactics then in use in Vietnam. We had also introduced into combat most of the weapons systems in use. When the Army developed a new piece of equipment, we were selected to test it, and if appropriate, develop the tactics for its employment in combat. By mid 1965, I had become one of the more experienced fire team leaders in the company, so was often selected to participate in the tests.

Some of the items that I was directly involved in testing included a bullet detector, a 40 millimeter nose mounted cannon, a .50 caliber door gun, a door mounted searchlight and the tear gas dispenser system I described earlier. Some of these items succeeded and some failed.

The idea for a bullet detector did not originate with us. It was welcomed as something that might prove useful. We knew that bullets often passed without our notice because a helicopter is a noisy machine in flight. (Most of us who flew them now need hearing aids). The only hint that we were being fired upon was the sound of the bullets as they hit the aircraft or passed very near (a hit was a 'whack' and a near miss was a 'pop'). At night we could see muzzle flashes and follow tracer rounds as they passed by our aircraft.

Industry had developed a device intended to alert us to the passing of a bullet anywhere in the vicinity of the aircraft. It consisted of a set of small antennas that were mounted on the outside of the aircraft, and a black box in the cockpit that was connected to an indicator on the instrument panel. The device would sense the sound waves of the passing bullet, flash a light on the instrument panel, put a beep in the earphones and record the event on a digital counter that kept track of how many bullets were detected.

The first few times I tried this device I disregarded it because it would frequently give an alarm over what I thought were friendly areas. I attributed these numerous alerts to faulty equipment that was detecting flight noises generated by the aircraft. The manufacturer's representative that had installed the device kept turning the sensitivity down and assuring me that it was working correctly. Further testing on fixed wing aircraft confirmed that the device was working, and that we were in fact being shot at every time it beeped. We were shocked at the frequency of fire coming from areas we thought to be under friendly control. Apparently half of the rice farmers in Vietnam were taking pot shots at us. Fortunately, they did not know how to aim at a helicopter. I think they underestimated our speed and consistently failed to take proper lead (aim far enough in front of us).

The bullet detector was eventually mounted on most helicopters in Vietnam. However I suspect a lot of crews did what the crews in our unit did with it. We almost never turned it on. We found that the frequent alarms interrupted our focus with information that we could do nothing about. In retrospect, this large amount of previously undetected ground fire was an early hint that the 'Pacification Program,' and the war itself, was not going as well as our politicians and military leaders were telling the American public.

A shoulder fired, single shot 40 millimeter grenade launcher had been developed for ground troops several years before the Vietnam War. It extended the range that a soldier could toss a grenade from about fifty feet out to several hundred feet. Our door gunners often carried one of these weapons and occasionally used it on bunkers and area targets. The rate of fire was severely restricted. It looked like a single barreled, large caliber shotgun, and fired a low velocity round. It had to be pointed well above the gun-target sight line in order to 'lob' the round into the target. This upward pointing of the barrel is called 'super elevation.'

In the early 1960s the Army decided to develop a rapid firing version of this weapon. This new one fired like a slow machine gun. It also had a longer range and a bigger warhead than the shoulder fired version. The aircraft version, named the M-5, was mounted in a pod on the nose of the helicopter. Designed to be fired by the copilot using a movable sight, it could be aimed left, right and under the helicopter. The hump the 40 millimeter system made on the nose of the aircraft reminded someone of a frog, so we named it the 'Frog.' These aircraft were also armed with pods of 2.75 inch aerial rockets.

In May 1965 our unit received the first systems to arrive in country, and my fire team was selected to participate in early combat testing. My first challenge was to figure out how to safely fly the aircraft with it mounted. The extra weight significantly altered the center of gravity of the aircraft, and influenced the airflow around it. Once this was mastered, I had to figure out how to best use it in combat.

I flew to a nearby free fire training area and my copilot fired several loads of ammunition in different modes of flight (slow, fast, in climb, in descent, in various turns). We quickly found out that it was nearly impossible for the copilot to be accurate with first rounds. He had to 'walk' the rounds onto the target in a manner similar to the way you would adjust a water hose on a spot on the ground. Therefore, we decided that it was a good 'area' weapon with which to rip up the jungle, but not much good for point targets and close air support for ground troops. We were not impressed.

As an afterthought at the end of our training missions I tried firing the Frog from the pilot's seat. This was accomplished by firing the weapon in a stowed forward position. In that mode, it was aimed by aiming the aircraft. The difference in firing stowed 40 MM and stowed machine guns is that you had to pull the nose of the aircraft well above the horizontal to lob the grenades. Thus, the pilot's fixed gun sight was useless and accuracy was nearly impossible. After a few failed attempts, it occurred to me that as the nose of the aircraft was pointed more and more downward, the grenades would require less and less super elevation.

Before I proceed, I need to point out that the Huey was not designed to fly with its nose pointed toward the ground. This limitation was primarily due to the big flat plastic windshield, which was subject to shatter at speeds of over about one hundred and forty mph. Another limitation was something called 'blade stall' which occurred when the advancing rotor blade approached the speed of sound. This would flip the aircraft on its back with catastrophic results. Therefore, to point the nose sharply downward the aircraft had to first be slowed, then the nose-low attitude held only until the speed built up to a speed at which you could safely pull out of the dive before exceeding the speed redline.

By some experimentation I discovered that if I slowed to about fifty mph I could point the nose down at an angle of about thirty degrees for about twenty seconds. This was enough time to fire a long burst of 40 millimeter then pull out without exceeding the red line. I also learned to use a grease pencil marker to place an X on the windshield in front of me where the impacting rounds appeared. By repeating the same flight profile, and holding my head in the same position, I had a workable sight for the rounds. I had found a way to be accurate against point targets with this new weapon.

On my first combat mission in a Frog I was directed by ground troops to attack a building that had a concrete tile roof. A squad of

Vietcong had taken refuge inside. I decided to try the 40 millimeter and it worked beautifully. During the first dive I got a full burst of about one hundred grenades on the roof. The explosions completely removed the roof from the building. My wingman followed with rockets and machine guns and finished the job. This high dive angle and other techniques we developed were to become standard maneuvers with units throughout Vietnam as they received their frogs. Ultimately, the 40 millimeter proved to be a reliable and successful helicopter weapon and was to be part of the armament on the first AH-1G Cobras that were built a few years later.

The same month we received the Frog we began testing a door mounted searchlight that was built locally in Vietnam. It consisted of a cluster of seven aircraft landing lights that were mounted in the right door of a helicopter. The center light was fixed but the six surrounding lights were coupled and could be moved to 'focus' at various distances. Collectively, these seven lights created over a million candle power, and could light up an area the size of a football field, or focus down on a single building. This lighting system was named 'Lightning Bug,' and was used almost nightly for the remainder of the war.

To help protect the Lightning Bug we decided to find a way to mount a heavy machine gun on one of our helicopters. The metal shop welded up a stand that bolted to the floor in the right cargo door (pilot's side). On top of it they attached a swivel mount for a fifty caliber machine gun. The door gunner, tied to the aircraft by what we called a 'monkey strap,' stood behind the gun and fired as the pilot circled the target.

In about July 1965 my fire team was placed on night flight duties for several weeks. Our mission was to fly with Lightning Bug on night patrols of the rivers and canals west of Saigon in an effort to slow the movement of enemy soldiers and equipment. Up until that time the enemy was moving freely at night throughout the area. This mission turned out to be the most successful and rewarding one of my entire first year in Vietnam.

Night flying became routine and even preferable to day missions. Although the odds were against making a safe emergency landing at night, there was considerably less ground fire with which to contend. We would place tape over the bottom half of our running lights so we would be visible from above by other aircraft, but not from below by the enemy. Also, the Vietcong could not figure out how to correctly estimate range and aim at our aircraft at night.

After a bit of experimentation we settled on a set of Lightning Bug tactics. The aircraft carrying the light would fly at about one thousand feet above the ground. My fire team would fly behind and slightly below the light, and I usually had the platoon leader supporting me from above in his Hog. The fifty caliber ship would fly higher and off to the side of the light.

To initiate the mission we would wait near our aircraft at the airfield until enemy movements were detected by outposts or airborne radar and reported to us by radio. It would take us about five minutes to 'scramble' into the air and another few minutes to fly to the area of reported activity. Upon arrival, the Lightning Bug would turn on his light, usually surprising the enemy. We could clearly see the boats with their crews looking at the light like deer caught in a car's headlights.

The enemy was always well armed but all they could see was the searchlight. They would concentrate their antiaircraft fire on him but almost never got hits. Once the enemy opened fire we could see the source of their green tracers (friendly tracers are orange). The first firing pass was almost too easy since they did not know we were there. On subsequent passes, the enemy returned fire, sometimes with success.

My most memorable Lightning Bug mission occurred on the night of 9-10 August 1965. The mission went exactly as outlined above until the light was turned on. There before us was a whole fleet of fifty or more sampans. They ranged in length from fifteen to thirty feet, and were loaded with men, supplies and equipment. This was obviously a major enemy unit movement.

This particular night I was flying a frog. As I started shooting I immediately began receiving heavy fire. The green tracers going by our aircraft looked as big as refrigerators. I made several firing passes and had almost expended my ammunition when my aircraft took hits in the radio compartment. A small electrical fire was started, so I turned toward our home airfield, hoping to get the aircraft on the ground before it burned. The wind blowing through the bullet holes in the nose blew out the fire, so we continued on and safely landed. My radios were out and my lights were off, so for a time, my wingman and platoon leader thought I had gone down. They were happy to find me in one piece back at the airfield when they arrived. I got another aircraft and as soon as everybody was rearmed and refueled, returned to the battle.

We found the enemy scrambling around trying to recover equipment from the river and reorganize their flotilla. We attacked again and again. Using up our ammunition, we returned to rearm two more times before the night was over. On the last attack I took hits through my windshield but was again lucky that none of my crew was seriously wounded. We all got some cuts from flying plastic, which qualified us for the Purple Heart Medal, but none of us ever bothered to apply for it.

The next day friendly ground forces went to the area and reported that most of the boats had been sunk or damaged. A large amount of equipment was destroyed, and there had been many enemy casualties in the engagement. As a result of this battle my platoon leader, Bill Fraker, recommended my crew and me for awards. I was presented with the Silver Star Medal prior to my departure from Vietnam. The Army Times, a military newspaper distributed worldwide, reported details of this engagement. The recognition from the article was to follow me to my next assignment and beyond.

CHAPTER 9

MISSION ACCOMPLISHED

One of the strangest events I experienced during the war occurred in September 1965 involving free-fire zones (FFZ). My fire team and another one from another platoon had attacked different targets near the same FFZ on the same day. Upon our return to the unit at the end of the day, we found a Colonel from higher headquarters there looking for the team that had engaged a target in or near the FFZ. To our consternation, he was investigating the shooting of a group of friendly civilians. A Vietnamese district chief had complained that some of his friendly villagers had been attacked.

We always lived in fear of shooting friendly civilians. In addition to not wanting to hurt innocent people, we did not want to expose our selves to disciplinary action. The investigating officer in this case was surprised to find two teams that admitted to possibly making the attack. This started a multi-day, extensive investigation during which I was on pins and needles. As it turned out, both teams were exonerated, but not because they didn't shoot and not because civilians were not killed. In fact, two groups of people had been attacked with deadly results.

The group that had complained was found to have been wrongly inside of the FFZ, so they had no grounds to complain, and no further action was required. The other group was outside the FFZ but that group was found to be Vietcong. Again, there were no grounds for further action. Both Teams were extremely relieved to see the investigation concluded with favorable results. This was the one and only investigation in which I was involved, and needless to say, I was extremely reluctant to operate near the boundaries of FFZs for the remainder of my tour.

Another bizarre event occurred shortly after the FFZ debacle. I was leading my fire team across a known enemy jungle area east of Saigon. We were flying at fifteen hundred feet and were occasionally receiving small arms fire. I had the gun circuit breakers inserted, which activated the switches on the control sick used to fly the aircraft. I passed control to the copilot while I reached for a clipboard on which my map was mounted. As I moved the clipboard into my lap I accidentally hit the rocket fire switch. Two rockets fired, startling the entire crew.

Since we were flying straight and level, the rockets flew off into the distance and impacted out of our sight. I had no idea where they had landed. I could do nothing about the situation so continued on our flight path. A few minutes later I heard a panicked radio call reporting several friendly casualties and two smoking holes. I was frozen with shock. There could be no doubt that the two holes were caused by my rockets.

I pondered what I should do. Offer to evacuate wounded? That might reveal my involvement. I discussed it with my copilot and we agreed that the truth would eventually come out. With a heavy heart, I turned toward where I suspected our rockets landed. Then out of the blue, I was saved again. An American voice came on the radio and said that a flight of Vietnamese bombers had accidentally dropped two bombs on a friendly patrol just east of where we were operating. I was off the hook and had again learned a hard lesson. My level of attention to cockpit circuit breakers and switch positions was forever intensified.

During the early months of my tour we used Army rocket pods that were built out of metal and were reusable. For some reason, in about August 1965 we began to be issued U.S. Air Force pods that were designed for one use. Fighter jets routinely jettison their pods after they fired the missiles. These new pods, which were painted white, were made out of cardboard. We found that they could be used more than once unless they got wet. We were authorized to jettison empty pods on the way home from a mission if the pods malfunctioned or if we had flown through rain.

There were designated areas around Saigon where we could safely drop these pods. I quickly learned how to make a grand game out of dumping used rocket pods. As I flew back from a mission at fifteen hundred feet I would select a target and try to 'bomb' it with the empty pods. There was a button on the pilot's control stick that allowed us to electrically drop the pods.

The drop point was a mere guess by the pilot. We were never really accurate but I do recall one time when my two pods hit on either side of a sampan. It was floating down a canal in the center of a designated drop area so it was fair game. As the pods descended, a couple of people stuck their heads out from the small shelter in the center of it. Imagine their surprise when those large white 'bombs' hit, splashing water over them. I bet they are still talking about the day the bombs did not go off.

At about this point in my tour I began to help train a new crop of fire team leaders. They would fly with me in the left (copilot's) seat for a few days then move to the right seat. When I felt they were ready I would send them to fly with the platoon instructor pilot for a check ride.

Finally, one showed up that was advertised as my eventual replacement. He name was Lieutenant Jim Moody, and he proved to be a good one. Jim was an unusually tall and fit officer with a sparkling personality. He became a great fire team leader and survived his tour. Unfortunately for the Army, he got out of the Army to become a Special Agent with the Federal Bureau of Investigation. Before retirement he would rise to the very top of the Bureau, serving for several years as a Deputy Director.

During the time I was training Jim I was assigned several missions to support the insertion and extraction of long range reconnaissance patrol (LRRP) operations. I would take about five heavily armed Americans and drop them in an isolated location in the jungle. I would put them on the ground just before dark, and take them out just after daylight several days later. Sometimes they never came back. In order to confuse the enemy as to where I dropped them off, I would land several places in the area and stay on the ground for only a few seconds. During one of these landings the patrol would jump out of the aircraft and I would proceed to land and take off at a few other places.

This was probably my least favorite mission because it required me to violate almost every Cardinal Rule. Each time I landed during the insertions I was completely vulnerable to being shot down. I was clearly operating in or near enemy controlled territory. During extractions there was almost always enemy nearby that were chasing the LRRP.

On the last LRRP mission that I flew I approached an area to recover a team that had been inserted a few days earlier. I had been given a time and place to make the pickup but had no radio contact with them. As I approached a rice paddy near the pick up point I observed a person standing in the middle of it. He was wearing a poncho and big hat. Thinking he might be one of the LRRPs, I approached cautiously. As I slowed and dropped through about one hundred feet, he simultaneously threw off the hat, pushed up the poncho and aimed an AK-47 at us. One of my door gunners shot him before he could fire it.

As I nosed the aircraft over to regain altitude and airspeed I observed two more people coming out of the tree line. They had no hats and were waving their arms at me. I again made a cautious approach. They turned out to be two of the five LRRPs for which I was looking. The remainder had been killed or captured, and all of the team's radios had been destroyed. They jumped on board and as we lifted off, we came under fire from the tree line and barely escaped. A few days later the LRRP support mission was picked up by another unit, and I was glad to see it go. I never understood what motivated those brave Americans to risk it all in the jungle. Of course, they considered us crazy to fly helicopters since we had essentially nothing to protect us but an aluminum skin about as thick as a beer can.

It was fitting that my final mission as a fire team leader be flown in support of a medical evacuation mission involving a Dustoff aircraft. On the morning of 1 October 1965 I reported to a special forces camp near the city of Tay Ninh, about seventy miles northeast of Saigon. My fire team was one of two from our unit assigned to provide fire support for a ground operation. Upon arrival I found a Dustoff aircraft already there. On kidding the crew about unshaven faces, I found out that they had been there all night.

I refueled and took off to begin our mission. The other Playboy fire team remained on the ground to be ready to assist and eventually replace me we I got low on fuel. The plan was to rotate the fire teams so that the friendly troops would constantly have immediate support. I soon arrived over the supported unit and got a briefing on the radio. The unit consisted of about two hundred South Vietnamese special forces troops with American advisors. They were making a sweep through rice paddies at the foot of Nui Ba Dinh Mountain.

The mountain rose almost vertically out of the surrounding rice paddies and was over three thousand feet tall. The Vietcong controlled the sides of the mountain while American forces had a radio relay station on the very top. South Vietnamese troops had been trying for months to dislodge the enemy with no success.

About ten minutes after my arrival the friendly unit was suddenly pinned down by intense fire. The Vietcong were dug in on the almost vertical sides of the mountain and were firing directly down on the Vietnamese. I began an attack but seeing that the Vietcong were well dug in, I immediately called for the assistance of the other fire team. Making repeated passes on the sides of the mountain, I had completely expended my ammunition when the other team arrived. They ripped into the enemy positions immediately, using their ammunition sparingly in an attempt to sustain the attack until I could service my aircraft and return.

While I was rearming and refueling, the other team was contacted by the ground troops stating that they had several wounded and requested an immediate medical evacuation helicopter. As I cranked my engine to take off, I relayed the message to Dustoff. He took off just behind me and followed me to the battle area.

Realizing that the other team was low on fuel and ammunition, I radioed that I would escort Dustoff. I slid in behind him and turned all weapons systems to the ready position. I announced the plan on the radio. I told the other team to maintain a one thousand feet orbit and place what fire they could down on the enemy. I would escort Dustoff until he landed, then remain at tree top level and shoot directly into the positions on the side of the mountain. With four helicopters attacking from two directions I hoped to keep the Vietcong's heads down and weapons quiet until Dustoff was safely airborne.

As Dustoff landed, not two hundred feet from the side of the mountain, I started a left hand orbit around the defenseless aircraft. This allowed one of my team's two aircraft to keep in firing position at all times. On my second orbit gunfire shattered my windshield and filled the cockpit with a white cloud of flying plastic. I radioed Dustoff that we were receiving heavy fire and asked him to make it snappy. He reported that he had one more patient to load, and would be ready in thirty seconds. On the third orbit my wingman reported receiving several hits. As I rolled around again I expected to see Dustoff taking off but he was still stationary.

Dustoff had found another wounded American and needed a few more seconds. I called the fire team that was in high orbit and told them to come on down if they had any ammunition left. I reported that both my choppers were out of ammunition. I began to wonder about my aircraft when the crew chief reported bullet holes in the engine compartment. My flight controls were getting stiff so I started to swing away from the battle and head for a forced landing area. However, I was diverted when Dustoff announced he was ready to come out.

I climbed and circled, hoping to draw some fire away from Dustoff and the other fire team as they come out low and fast. As the flight started out they were informed that another wounded American had been found and requested Dustoff come back. Once more Dustoff went back into the deadly enemy fire. This one was quick, and he took off almost as soon as he landed. The four gunships had expended every bit of their ammunition.

Back on the ground Dustoff reported that he had not received a single hit. The other fire team leader found three holes in his aircraft and both of my aircraft were down about three miles from the operational area, damaged beyond immediate repair. Dustoff had the prizes. He had evacuated two Americans and three Vietnamese. All five were to survive because of the teamwork and intense devotion to duty of the crewmembers of the five aircraft involved.

In October 1965 during my last mission as a fire team leader an armor piercing AK-47 bullet passed through this hole, forcing me to land.

As a footnote to this story, I was able to get and keep the bullet that entered the windshield and passed just over my head. It grazed my helmet, and entered the transmission causing loss of oil pressure. This and a loss of hydraulic pressure forced me to make an emergency landing. Without oil pressure the transmission would lock up, and the rotor blades would stop going around with obvious results. Without hydraulic pressure the aircraft becomes very difficult to control. In this case, I was able to get on the ground without any further damage.

Looking back on the battle I realized that the good old 13th Cardinal Rule had saved my life again. I had instinctively tried to complicate the Vietcong's marksmanship by not attacking directly into their guns. Rather than fly straight at their positions on the side of the mountain while shooting, I had placed the aircraft in a slight descent and a slight turn. If I had been straight and level, the round that went over my head could have struck me between the eyes.

As stated earlier, this was my final combat mission on my first tour. My platoon leader, Captain Bill Fraker, said this mission used up what little luck I had left, and made me 'hang up my jockey strap' in the bar at our lounge. It was tradition in the unit at that time that when a pilot completed his last mission his name would be written on an actual (new) athletic jockey strap. It was then hung with others on the wall in the unit lounge.

With the pressure of daily missions relaxed I began to enjoy life again. One night in October a group of pilots with musical talent got together to record some of their home grown songs. The songs were sung to the tunes of folk music. However, the words had been changed to relate, sometimes with grim humor, the reality of day to day combat flying.

Warrant Officer Mike Davis, a wingman in another Playboy fire team, was the lead singer. His all time favorite song had been written in Saigon in 1964 by then Lieutenant Bob Matlick, a fire team leader in our company. It was sung to the tune of 'Big Iron,' a country and western song by Marty Robbins. Bob's words became popular and the song was eventually designated 'The UTT Song.' Copies of Mike's recording are available through the 145th Combat Aviation Battalion Vietnam Association, and as of 2005, Mike was still singing it at UTT and 145th Aviation Battalion reunions. The words are self-explanatory.

THE UTT SONG 'THE TEST'

**To the flight line hear in Saigon; a new pilot came one day.
He didn't talk to folks around him; didn't have too much to say.
Did he dare to ask a question? Did he dare to make a slip?
For he knew that for the first time; he had weapons on his ship.
Weapons on his ship.
Now it was early in the morning and the crew chief wore a frown.
He didn't know if the new replacement could get his chopper off the ground.
He knew this was deadly business and there couldn't be a slip.
And he knew a fledgling pilot could bring trouble to his ship.
Trouble to his ship.
Soon the pilot learned his lessons while flying all around.
He received his first baptism from the Vietcong on the ground.
Many rounds came through the cockpit; they struck the rotor head.
He looked around behind him; thinking' everyone was dead.
Everyone was dead.
He could see the gunner shootin'; he could hear the crew chief shout.
I can see them bastard runnin'; God that markin' smoke is out.
Before the Vietcong reached cover; his bullets fairly ripped.
And the wingman's aim was deadly with the weapons on his ship.
The weapons on his ship.
There was a hundred yards between them when he made his second pass.
He could hear machineguns chatter; he could feel the rockets blast.
He could see the rice fields burning and the gun smoke he could smell.
The fire he saw around him made him whisper holy hell.
Whisper holy hell.
Now it was over in a moment; there was silence all around.
As the bodies of the Vietcong lie before him on the ground.
He had survived his first encounter and just like all the rest.
Now he was a combat pilot who had passed the crucial test.
Passed the crucial test.**

Playboys on 10 September 1965. From left front Paxton, Murphy, me, Faker, and Clark. Standing from left Sheppard, Krofchek,, Burkett, ?, Kammerer, Moody, Rhoades and Dalton. Clark was killed the next night.

Band of brothers in 2003. From left Dick Jarrett, me and Bill Fraker. We all completed an Army career and retired as Colonels.

I had a few weeks left in country before I was due to depart. I spent the time writing some efficiency reports and awards for my fire team members. I also flew some 'ash and trash' missions, which included such exciting tasks as flying hot chow to forward deployed fire teams. For the first time in Vietnam I found myself flying at the outrageously high altitude of three thousand feet. It was a warm, comfortable feeling to just sit back and enjoy traveling from one secure area to another. During this period I discovered that Vietnam was a beautiful country.

My date of departure, 18 November 1965, suddenly arrived. I was just one of a couple of hundred people on the aircraft. When the wheels left the ground a huge cheer erupted. As we departed Vietnamese air space my thoughts momentarily turned to all of those that I had known who would not get to make this trip. Then it hit me. I was going to join my family and never see Vietnam again. I could hardly wait for my new life to begin. Little did I know that in about two years I would return for another tour.

CHAPTER 10

BETWEEN TOURS

We approached the good old U.S.A. before dawn. I anxiously peered out of the window to watch the beautiful lights of San Francisco grow in the distance. We landed at Travis Air Force Base. I boarded a bus for an hour ride to the San Francisco International Airport, where I bought a ticket to Nashville. Mary Jane met me and we had a joyous reunion. I spent a few days getting re-acquainted with my children. Bill remembered me but Nonna didn't. She looked at me from her crib with great suspicion for several days. This was a special time for my family and me because now Vietnam was behind us and the whole world was in front of us. Nobody had even heard of somebody having to go back to the war a second time.

A Cookeville Tennessee newspaper reporter came to our home and interviewed me length. His article, published in several area newspapers, called me a hero and quoted me as saying the war was getting tougher but we were winning. I really felt like I was appreciated.

A few days later we departed to visit my parents in Cleveland, Tennessee. During the automobile trip a rock flew out of a tire on a car in front us and hit our windshield. I was not yet deprogrammed from combat, and for a few seconds thought we were receiving fire. I almost hit the ditch as I ducked. Mary Jane could not figure out what was going on and it took me a few minutes to calm down enough to explain it to her.

In Cleveland I was again interviewed, and a newspaper article was published. I was invited by two local civic clubs to speak to them at their monthly luncheon, but had been told by the Army to not accept these types of invitations without clearing it with them first. I turned them down. In retrospect, that was a mistake. By the time I got home from my other tours in Vietnam, the war was so controversial that I never received another invitation.

Somewhere about the middle of my now completed Vietnam tour I had applied for a Regular Army Commission. It had been approved and along with it came orders to report to Ft. Sill, Oklahoma for the Artillery Officers Career Course. At that time the field artillery was combined with the air defense artillery as one branch. Therefore, the course I attended was in two parts, one part at Fort Sill for field artillery training and one part at Fort Bliss, Texas for air defense training.

I arrived at Fort Sill a few months early for my scheduled class, so was temporarily assigned to a provisional unit that was experimenting with firing rockets from CH-34 helicopters. This was the same aircraft that I had flown in flight school, so I had no trouble getting re-qualified. The rocket, however, was a different matter. The type rocket that I had employed in Vietnam was equipped with fins that folded out after launch to stabilize it in flight. Think of it as an arrow.

The new rocket had no fins. Its rocket motor exhaust was used to spin it in flight, thus providing stabilization. Think of this one as a bullet. The new one required a totally different technique to achieve accuracy. After a time I was able to master it. Over the next several months I participated in many training exercises and performed several demonstration firings for various groups of visitors.

During this period I was introduced to the Army's tendency to over prepare for an important event. We were scheduled to fire a demonstration for about thirty members of the U.S. Congress. We had to prepare a field site from which they could view the show. Someone decided that they needed bathroom facilities. So, we installed the standard field artillery men's field urinal, which consisted of a three feet long cardboard ammunition tube stood on end with the bottom in the ground. We put in four. It was later decided we needed twelve. When the Commanding General came out to check the adequacy of our preparations, he decided that there was a chance that all thirty of the Congressmen would need to go to the bathroom at the same time. So we put in a total of thirty tubes. To my knowledge, none of them were ever used. I had learned another lesson for later in life.

The course started on 8 February 1966. It was a challenge for me because I had never studied gunnery or nuclear weapons employment, both of which were central to the course. Neither had I received formal training on adjusting artillery fire although I had employed it dozens of times in combat.

I was one of the few students to have been to Vietnam, and was treated with respect and some deferment. This is best illustrated by an example. During my first attempt to adjust live artillery on the firing range, I accurately calculated the location of the target and radioed the map coordinates to the fire direction center. The first rounds hit very near the target. I ordered the guns to "add fifty feet and fire for effect" The rounds came out and hit right on the target.

The other students around me looked perplexed. I assumed they were in awe of my great shooting skills. However, one of them whispered to me that I had just failed the shoot because I had not bracketed the target before firing for effect. The field artillery has an unbendable rule that a target has to be bracketed (rounds land both long and short) before firing all six guns for effect. I should have added one hundred feet and fired another set of adjusting rounds, then dropped fifty feet to hit the target. The instructor was aware that I had fired artillery numerous times in Vietnam. He asked me if that was the way we had done it in over there. I replied yes, that we could not afford to waste rounds in combat. He took pity on me and gave me a passing grade. I am sure that if anyone else in the class had adjusted as I had, he would have failed.

While at Fort Sill I flew about four hours per month in an OH-13 Sioux, which was like the first helicopter I had seen while still in college. I spent the flying time taking my new non-aviator friends up and teaching them a little about helicopters. I took great care in flying safely because a few months earlier a flight school classmate and former member of my unit in Vietnam was killed at Fort Sill. He had been flying as copilot in an U-6 Beaver when its wing hit a pole and crashed. He was not even fixed wing rated. What a waste!

About half way through the course I received orders for my follow-on assignment. I was disappointed to find out that I was going to a new aviation unit that was to be formed at Fort Bragg, North Carolina. I was strongly suspicious that it would eventually deploy to Vietnam. That all changed a few weeks later when I got the most important telephone call I would ever get while in the Army.

The Bell Helicopter Company in Fort Worth, Texas had built an armed helicopter that was unlike anything the world had ever seen. They took the dynamic components (engine/transmission/rotor/drive train) of the Huey and wrapped them in an airframe that was only about three feet wide. It looked something like a jet fighter. It was known as the Huey Cobra. Bell offered to build it for the Army. After some testing, the Army decided to buy several hundred of them and send them to Vietnam.

The two officers in the Pentagon that were managing the acquisition of these new gunships just happened to be my former company commanders in Vietnam, Major Jaggers and Major Booth. They had selected my initial UTT platoon leader, Captain Jarrett (now a Major), to select the pilots that would take the first few aircraft to Vietnam. I received a telephone call from him one day while home from class having lunch. At the first sound of his voice a cold chill went down my back. For a brief moment I found myself back in the cockpit in Vietnam.

After a friendly discussion and a little background about the Army's plans for the Cobra, he popped the question. Would I be interested in being assigned to the project? I accepted without hesitation. He told me details would have to be worked out with my branch, and that I would receive new orders soon. He later told me that I was the first person he called with an offer. I took that as a great complement.

In a few days I received orders to report to the flight school at Fort Rucker to attend instrument qualification training and instructor pilot training. Following that, I was to report to the Bell Helicopter Plant in Fort Worth, Texas, to serve as a test pilot and assist in the building of the first few aircraft. Of course, I had to complete my artillery training before embarking on this dream assignment.

I finished at Fort Sill and went to Fort Bliss for a few weeks to complete the air defense portion of the course. While there I maintained my flying proficiency in my old friend from initial flight training, the OH-23 Raven. El Paso is located several thousand feet above sea level.

Helicopters do not fly well at that altitude due to the thin air. When I got my checkout in the aircraft, I was told not to expect to save the aircraft in the event of an engine failure. The best I could hope for was to walk away from the crash site.

We enjoyed our return to Texas. We especially enjoyed shopping in Mexico, and eating the great Mexican food found in El Paso. We liked the clear, clean air and the mountains so much that we actually discussed returning there to retire someday. We later dropped that plan after we lived in Hawaii, California and a few other neat places. What we never planned was is retire in Tennessee. In the end, family ties overrode all of our preferences, and we went back to our roots.

Around Christmas 1966 I completed my training at Fort Rucker and reported to the Bell Helicopter Plant. We had moved four times that year. All we had to do was put the children's blankets on their beds and they were 'home.'

I was the first member of the Cobra New Equipment Training Team (NETT) to arrive, so was temporarily assigned to a small Army office in the plant that coordinated the Army's inspection and acceptance of new aircraft. That office consisted of several administrative persons and two test pilots. I joined the test pilots and was trained by them to perform what was called an 'acceptance test flight.'

The Bell Plant assembled the helicopters. When they were completed and rolled out the door, Bell test pilots would then fly them to check out and fine tune all of the systems, instruments and radios. Once a new aircraft was deemed ready for delivery to the Army, one of the Army test pilots would fly the aircraft for a minimum of one hour. We had a long, formal list of things to check out. If we found anything wrong, Bell would fix it and we would check it again. When everything met our standards, the test pilot signed an acceptance form. At that point the Army owned the aircraft.

The senior Army test pilot was Captain Nick Stein. He was the best helicopter pilot with which I ever flew. He taught me things about flying that I thought impossible. We would go out to an isolated airfield and compete to see who could stretch a simulated forced landing the greatest distance. He always won. The training Nick gave me was to save my life about a year later in Vietnam when an engine blew up on takeoff.

In about February 1967 the manufacturer of the engine for the Huey, the Lycoming Company, experienced a strike by its workers. Due to the ongoing war, Bell Helicopter could not afford to stop their production line. Nick and I were tasked to fly each new aircraft to a nearby Army depot. There the engine was removed and shipped back to the Bell plant where it was put back on the production line. This procedure was repeated for several weeks until the strike was over. At that point we had several dozen aircraft without engines in storage. Later, as engine production caught up, Nick and I had to go to the depot and test fly all of the aircraft with their new engines. I never understood how a union could strike in the middle of a war. I have not held unions in very high esteem since.

Nick was also a fixed wing rated pilot. He took me for a ride in a National Guard O-1 Bird Dog. It was the smallest of all Army aircraft, seating only two people, one behind the other. We were flying over the outskirts of Fort Worth when Nick decided to demonstrate a stall maneuver. He pulled the power back and the nose up until the aircraft quit flying. It suddenly shuddered and the nose pointed straight down. Nick was able to pull it out of the dive but we were only a few feet over the trees. I didn't know anything was wrong but Nick later told me that he almost lost it. He had been doing stalls without a passenger, and had not counted on my extra weight. This was the second time I was almost killed while trusting somebody else at the controls of an aircraft. The first had occurred in flight school when Cadet An almost flew into the ground while trying to land a CH-34 at night.

During this time I would spend part of my day on the Bell assembly line watching the first Cobras being built. I was consulted frequently on cockpit configuration and armament switch and circuit breaker placements. Also, I started my checkout in the prototype Cobra. Since there was no Army instructor pilots yet qualified, I received my training from the Bell test pilots.

After five hours of flying time I completed my check-out in the Cobra, and became the first Army pilot to be rated in it. I felt like a true member of the Bell team. The aircraft in which I trained was known as 209J. That was the Bell designation for it, and that number was painted on the tail fin. The aircraft had been hand built by Bell at their own expense, then demonstrated to the Army. A unique feature of the aircraft was that it had retractable skids. The Army decided that the retraction mechanism added too much weight to the aircraft, so didn't buy that feature. I saw the aircraft in about 1986 in the museum at Fort Knox, Kentucky. I don't know why it didn't end up in the Army Aviation Museum at Fort Rucker. I think it should have.

The first Cobras did not have a crew compartment air conditioning system. The Army did not want to install them due to the weight they would add to the aircraft. During our early flights inside the completely closed canopy we found that the cockpit temperature would soar to well over one hundred degrees. Because of our complaints, the Army directed Bell to conduct some experiments to examine pilot proficiency at high cockpit temperatures. You guessed it! I was one of the guinea pigs.

Bell built a mock-up Cobra cockpit inside a hanger and equipped it with a temperature control system and lots of instrumentation. I would sit in it and perform routine cockpit functions for an hour and a half at a time. This was the average flight time of a typical mission. These sessions were repeated for various temperatures and the degradation of my skills measured and compared. These experiments alone were unsuccessful in justifying air conditioning. They were successful, however, in making me wish I was in a different business.

The Army's initial fix for the hot cockpit was to tint the Plexiglas canopy blue. This helped a little but we soon learned that the tint greatly restricted our visibility at night. Also, during night firing the flash of the weapons reflected off of the canopy and almost blinded us.

After we arrived in Vietnam the cockpit heat problem got worse. We would come back from a mission and be soaking wet with sweat. Finally, we started weighing ourselves before and after each mission. We found that we temporarily lost an average of five pounds of weight per flight. We reported this up the chain of command but nothing was done. Finally, we invited an Army Aviation General to fly with us. He almost crashed when some sweat ran down into his eyes. Soon afterwards, new aircraft coming off of the production line were equipped with air conditioning. However, in keeping with the ways of the Army, it was not called air conditioning but was called an 'Environmental Control Unit (ECU).' Unfortunately, we had to complete our tour in the older aircraft, and I never flew an ECU equipped aircraft.

Sometime in March I was tasked to take a helicopter to the University of Texas and give orientation flights to their ROTC students. This was part of an effort to encourage youngsters to apply for flight school when they went on active duty. On this particular day I was flying a brand new aircraft just off of the production line. We arrived on campus early and shut the aircraft down. Following a habit developed in Vietnam to look over my aircraft after every landing, I climbed on top of the helicopter and started looking over the rotor head. To my horror, I noticed that one of the rotating components had a huge crack in it.

I called the Bell Plant to report the problem and was told to stand by, they were sending another aircraft and some mechanics to fix it. They arrived in a couple of hours. I used the replacement aircraft to complete my mission while the Bell personnel replaced the defective part. On return to the plant, engineers conducted some tests on the cracked part and determined that it would have broken early into the next flight, resulting in catastrophic loss of aircraft, crew and passengers. All Hueys worldwide were grounded and inspected, and the manufacturing process for the part was changed. Once again, attention to detail had saved my life and no telling how many more.

At the end of March 1967, I was reassigned from the Bell Plant to the Cobra NETT, and assumed the position of Executive Officer. The other members reported for duty at about the same time. We located ourselves in a National Guard hanger in Grand Prairie, a suburb of Fort Worth. Our mission became clear about that time. We were to prepare to take the first six aircraft, along with a maintenance support package, to Vietnam. Once there, we were to simultaneously test the aircraft, develop combat tactics, and train pilots from units in Vietnam that were going to be issued Cobras.

The Commander of the Cobra NETT was a Transportation Corps Aviator named Major Paul Anderson. Major Jarrett was the Deputy Commander. Major Anderson focused on the maintenance aspects of the aircraft and managed the funding. Major Jarrett focused on tactics and flight training, and ran the day to day operations. The team consisted of thirteen officers, twenty five enlisted and several civilians. The only Officer not selected by Major Jarrett was Captain Nick Stein. He was selected by Major Anderson and appointed as our maintenance officer.

Chief Warrant Officer John Thompson (in cockpit) and Captain Jim Pratt (left) and I discuss preparation of a Cobra for shipment to Vietnam in 1967

Captain Stein took advantage of his position as maintenance officer and put a huge new motorcycle in one of the cargo containers that his section was packing with aircraft spare parts to take to Vietnam. Once we got to Vietnam, he had instant transportation, which did not set well with the other team members. In about December 1967, Nick started to use the motorcycle to commute about twenty five miles to Saigon to live in a hotel. This eventually cost him his job, as I will describe later.

About half way through our year in Vietnam Major Anderson was promoted and departed to command an aviation battalion. Major Jarrett took command of the Team. I moved up to the Deputy Commander position, and when Major Jarrett departed a few months later, I took command. I had that job for about two months until my tour was over.

CHAPTER 11

SECOND TIME AROUND

In late August 1967 we loaded six Cobras and a Huey (our maintenance support aircraft), onto U.S. Air Force transports for the flight to Vietnam. We departed on 28 August and arrived at Bien Hoa Airfield on 30 August.

The day we arrived in Vietnam was the lowest day of my life to date. After all the excitement and hype of being part of something new and important, I suddenly realized that I was back in Vietnam for another whole year. That first night I sat in my room and my heart ached. I wrote a letter home, then decided I needed some kind of calendar on which I could count off the days. I drew up a 'short timer's calendar.' It was simply a piece of paper with three hundred and sixty five small squares on it. As the tour progressed, I would check off each day as it went by. I also recorded significant events. It became one of my most prized souvenirs.

Shortly after our arrival Dick Jarrett faced the toughest leadership problem he was to encounter during the year. The team was authorized six Jeeps, but we had seven claimants, five Captains and two Majors. Each of us wanted the prestige of having our own personal transportation. Dick came up with several distribution plans, but every one left somebody out. That person would cry on his shoulder, and he would try to find another solution. In one plan he actually gave up his own Jeep, but soon thought better of that, and took it back.

Dick finally solved the 'Great Jeep Problem' by deciding that Captain Jim Pratt, the armament officer, needed a pickup truck instead of a Jeep. I'm not sure how Jim ended up as the odd man out, but it probably had something to do with the fact that he was an Ordnance officer and had not been a member of the old UTT.

A few months later my Jeep was stolen when one of my Warrant Officers left it unlocked. It was last seen being driven into a CH-47 Chinook Helicopter belonging to the 1st Cavalry Division. I got the Military Police to write a report and our supply section was able to get me a brand new Jeep in one day. Such was the robustness of the supply system in Vietnam at that time.

Everybody wanted to be the first pilot to fly a Cobra in Vietnam, but Major Anderson took the honor himself, making the first flight on 31 August 1967. He took the maintenance officer, Nick Stein along as copilot. For the first month we worked on improving our maintenance area, training facilities and living quarters, and performed flights to perfect our combat tactics.

The Cobra was different from the Huey gunship in many ways. One of the most significant was that it had no door gunners. It also flew faster, dove at a steeper angle and had much more firepower. Another new capability was that we could rapidly reconfigure the weapons systems to fit the mission. Each wing had two bomb racks. All four racks could hold pods of nineteen rockets, or the inside racks could be used to carry mini-guns (a six barreled gun that could fire up to six thousand rounds per minute) and the outside racks rocket pods. In addition, the nose turret could carry two mini-guns, two grenade launchers, or one of each. The nose mounted mini-guns and grenade launchers could be aimed and fired by the copilot using his hand held sight. They could also be fired by the pilot in the fixed forward mode. The mini-guns were much more accurate than the rockets and grenades.

The inaccuracy of 2.75 inch rockets had been clearly demonstrated when one killed the Mayor of Saigon. A gunship from the gun platoon of another company fired several rockets at enemy targets while the Mayor and some of his staff watched. One of the rockets had a malfunction and deviated from its intended flight path, exploding near the group killing several of them. A big investigation was launched but the pilot was cleared of wrongdoing by the testimony of an American General Officer who happened to see the event.

Early in our efforts to figure out how to best fight with the Cobra, we found that we could perform a maneuver known as a 'wing over.' That is, we could roll in on a target just like a fighter jet. The maneuver was initiated by pulling the nose up and slowing down to about eighty mph, then rolling the aircraft almost inverted while letting the nose drop rapidly. After turning ninety degrees, we would roll out pointed at the target and open fire as we accelerated. The high dive angle greatly improved our accuracy. We had to initiate our turn away from the target at a fairly high altitude because of our rapidly building airspeed (two hundred and twenty mph maximum), and because we had no door gunners to protect us on the pull out.

The lack of door gunners prompted us to request a smoke dropping device so we could mark targets. It consisted of a tail mounted multi-barrel box containing several smoke grenades that could be dropped one at a time using a trigger in the cockpit. This device proved successful and allowed us to get smoke out when receiving fire as well as mark targets for U.S. fighter-bombers.

Another problem was the lack of cargo space that could be used for emergency evacuation of downed aircrews. To overcome this one we attached seat belts to the ammunition bay doors. When required, the doors could be opened and one person could ride to safety on each of the doors. Later in the Vietnam War, and even later in Iraq, this was successfully accomplished by having the downed crews simply straddle a rocket pod or wing and ride to safety.

To sharpen our gunnery skills, we shot up every target we could find in a free-fire zone nearby. We completed our own training and in late September started working with ten pilots from the first unit that was to be issued Cobras. That unit just happened to be my old platoon from the UTT, which by that time had been renamed the 334th Attack Helicopter Company. We completed their training on 7 October and shortly afterwards, their aircraft arrived and they became the first operational Cobra unit in history.

During our first months in Vietnam we conducted a publicity campaign, hoping to influence senior Army leadership in their acceptance of the Cobra. We gave demonstration rides to the overall commander, General Westmoreland, the Premier of Vietnam, General Ky and many others. The senior Army Aviator in Vietnam, Major General G.P. Seneff was taken for a flight on 4 September during which an enemy sampan was attacked and four Vietcong killed. He was given credit for the first Cobra kill of the war. He was also recognized as the first pilot qualified in Vietnam to fly the aircraft. To us underlings, this was a major case of sucking up to the boss. Such is how things are done in the Army.

I had the dubious honor of being the first pilot wounded in a Cobra. It happened on 31 January 1968. This was the first day of the Tet 1968 Vietcong offensive, which is considered by many to be the turning point of the war. Tet is a Vietnamese holiday when everybody goes to their home to visit relatives and celebrate the New Year Holiday. Each year up until this one the combatants, through mutual agreement, had taken a couple of weeks off during the holiday to celebrate. In 1968 the Vietnamese Army stood down but the Vietcong took advantage of them and launched a massive offensive.

Up until that point in the war the American people had been told that we were winning. Following the TET attack some of them began to lose faith in their political and military leadership simply because the Vietcong was able to launch the large scale Tet attack. They never understood (or cared) that the Vietcong was essentially wiped out during the battle. From then on, the bulk of the enemy consisted of North Vietnamese Regulars.

On the day before the attack we received intelligence reports about increased enemy activity and were placed on a higher state of alert. Things were quiet when I went to bed but just after midnight, I woke to the sound of loud explosions. The Bien Hoa Air Base was under rocket attack. At that time I was living with the other NETT Officers in an old three story hotel building in downtown Bien Hoa City, about two miles from the airfield. We all scrambled to the roof of the building to see what was going on. It was the most amazing fireworks display I had ever seen. As far as the eye could see in all directions the sky was filled with burning parachute flares. The Vietcong had launched a coordinated attack on literally every outpost and military base in the country. Incoming and outgoing rockets and mortars were exploding all around the airbase.

We were not under attack at our location, but we quickly got our pistols and rifles and prepared to defend our building. We anxiously watched the action until dawn. At that time the rocket attacks on the airbase had subsided, so we decided to jump in our Jeeps and try to make a run for the airfield and our aircraft. We left just after it got light and made the trip in about ten minutes. During the trip we were shot at from a water tower that overlooked the gate to the air base. Fortunately, none of us were hit but there were some bullet holes in the canvas top of my Jeep.

Our enlisted men, who lived on base, had our aircraft armed and ready to go. I took off and flew several combat missions that day. The first one took me low over the north side of Saigon where I was wounded by a round that came through the cockpit. The bullet hit an armored seat and split into two pieces. The smaller piece, the metal jacket, hit me in the back. I almost lost control of the aircraft but my copilot, Lieutenant Jim Lee, took over and got us safely back to the airfield. In my panic I embarrassed myself by using my first tour call sign, Playboy 1-1, on the radio. My Cobra NETT call sign was 'Striker 1-1.'

After some medical treatment I got another aircraft and returned to the fight. Twice during the day my aircraft malfunctioned and I had to return to the airfield and make emergency 'no tail rotor control' landings, which means that the pedals were frozen and I could not control the heading of the aircraft at slow speeds. I was able to make successful landings both times. The average pilot might have crashed, but I had been teaching other pilots how to make this type emergency landing, so my proficiency was very high.

On about the third mission over Saigon I received a request to attack several buildings in which the Vietcong were deployed. The target was a line of large one story wooden buildings in a densely populated area. They all looked alike and I suspected they were part of a military compound. The enemy had occupied the buildings and was dug in around them. The ground troops informed me that there were women and children close to the target buildings. Therefore, I decided to use only machine guns because they were more accurate than rockets.

I was flying my favorite aircraft that day. It was equipped with four mini-guns, two in the nose turret and one on each wing. The ammunition was configured so that every fifth round was a tracer round. The ammunition trays were fully loaded which gave me enough ammunition for about twenty seconds of continuous firing. That amount was sufficient for several bursts of two seconds length. I had to be absolutely sure of my accuracy so my plan was to disregard the Cardinal Rules and dive down to about five hundred feet, then fire the guns. At that range the tracers would still be burning when they entered the buildings. Therefore, I issued the following fire mission order to my wingman: "Striker 1-2 this Striker 1-1, fire mission, eight wooden buildings at my nine O'clock, west to east, mini-guns only, break left, over."

My wingman acknowledged the fire command and we rolled in at a steep angle from about one thousand feet. Sure enough, when the rounds hit it looked like a fly swatter hitting a pile of white bread flour. The buildings seemed to jump up off of the ground, and they immediately caught fire. The few Vietcong that made it out were rounded up by Vietnamese ground troops. Mission accomplished. This one became my all time favorite fire mission. For this and other actions that day, I was awarded my third Distinguished Flying Cross, and a Purple Heart medal.

I did not know it at the time but my old test pilot friend from Bell, Nick Stein, was on top of a hotel building nearby watching our attacks. He had been spending the nights before Tet in Saigon, and had been trapped there when the battle started. Somehow, he obtained a radio and all through the day he kept calling our operations center, pleading for them to send an aircraft to pick him up. He wanted to get in on the action, but was unsuccessful. It was a few days before he made it back to the unit. It was only a few days later that he was reassigned off of the NETT. You can guess why.

On one of my rearming and refueling stops I accidentally got Dick Jarrett's butt chewed by Major General Williams, our big boss. He was the senior Army Aviator in country, and had issued an order that all pilots would fly with their flight suit sleeves rolled down. This was a safety precaution intended to retard burns in case of a crash. I had been so busy that I completely forgot to roll mine down. Here we were

My favorite Cobra around Tet 1968. On the outboard wings are nineteen round rocket pods. On the inboard wings and in the nose turret are six barrel machine guns. During Tet two guns were installed in the nose turret.

in the middle of the fight of our lives, and this General comes up to my helicopter, looks me over, and tells me to roll my sleeves down. He then proceeded to take Dick off to the side and chew him royally. From then on it became part of our checklist to roll down our sleeves. We eventually had some elastic sewed into some cut off sleeves and simply slipped them up over our arms before take-off.

Later on that first day of the Tet Offensive, Warrant Officer Roger Cameron, a member of the first group of pilots we had trained, became the first Cobra pilot killed in action. Flying copilot in the front seat of a Playboy aircraft responding to a call for help, he was killed instantly when a round came through the windshield. I did not get all the details but it sounded like the pilot had intentionally or accidentally violated several Cardinal Rules and made the mistake of attacking a fifty caliber anti aircraft gun head on in the dead man zone.

Crew chief and armament specialist rearm between missions. They often competed with other crews to determine who was fastest.

We flew with sleeves rolled up until our General stopped us. The Cobra cockpit was very much like that of a fighter jet. The big difference was that it had no parachute, no ejection seat and no air conditioning.

As a result of the Tet Offensive we were required to move onto the airbase near our aircraft. We were lucky to get an abandoned U.S. Air Force compound into which we relocated. It consisted of two rows of one story wooden buildings with a separate bathroom building and a big bunker. Frequently after Tet the airbase siren would sound in the middle of the night, warning of incoming enemy fire. We were under orders to get into the bunker until the all clear was sounded. I soon got tired of these trips to that awful damp hole, and proceeded to build a bunker in my room. It was constructed of bags of sand under my bed, and was just big enough for me to squeeze into and go back to sleep. I took some flack from the guys but continued to use my private bunker until I finished my tour.

Some of the civilian technical representatives that were part of our team actually moved into and lived inside a bunker. They had been living with the enlisted soldiers in a two story barracks building. One night a large enemy rocket hit the building next door to theirs, killing and wounding several soldiers. That type of rocket was the most feared of the enemy ground attack weapons. It was about six feet long and as big around as a coffee can. Upon impact it would cause a tremendous explosion and was known to penetrate the roof of a bunker and kill everyone inside. We never felt safe during an attack, even inside a bunker.

The Tet battle lasted several days. Eventually, we resumed our training mission and continued to fly assigned combat missions, mostly at night. On one of these missions we were trying to find and attack the Vietcong along their infiltration routes north of Bien Hoa. This particular flight consisted of our Huey to drop parachute illumination flares, and three Cobras to do the shooting. I was the odd man out that night. It was my turn to fly the Huey. Nobody wanted that job so we took turns.

The Huey was loaded with one hundred magnesium flares, each one capable of producing about one million candle power of illumination for about five minutes. They were individually hooked to rip cords and tossed out the door by a door gunner. The parachute would open about one hundred feet below the aircraft, the flare would ignite, and the resulting light would slowly descend toward the ground. The reason nobody wanted to fly the Huey on this mission was that with all those flares onboard, it was a flying bomb. If it crashed it would explode and burn with enough energy to power a small city.

About one hour after sunset we took off. As my luck would have it, the Huey's engine blew up on initial takeoff from the airfield. I had gained about fifty feet of altitude and was accelerating through fifty mph when I heard a loud pop, the nose of the aircraft spun left, the instrument panel lit up with red and yellow lights and the warning buzzer went off in my headset. At that airspeed and altitude, an engine failure usually results in a crash because there is almost no reaction time. Fortunately, I was at my lifetime peak of proficiency in emergency operations. I had been performing and instruction others on engine failure landings for several months.

I was able to automatically take all of the correct actions to safely get the helicopter on the ground. Luckily, there was a clearing below me because there was no time to turn. As I completed the landing the tower called to say that there was fire coming out of my engine. It had literally disintegrated internally. We stepped out of the aircraft and counted our blessings. Needless to say, it was about twenty four hours before I was ready to fly again. This turned out to be the only complete engine failure I was to encounter in over three thousand hours of flying helicopters, and it was enough!

Another near miss occurred during a B-52 support mission. I failed to pick up the warning of the impending strike and was flying at about one thousand feet over the target area when the flight of B-52s flew over me and dropped their bombs. Their route came directly toward me so the impacts started to my front and progressed toward and on either side of me. I immediately knew what was going on but did not know what action to take. This time, doing nothing proved correct. I was high enough to escape damage to my aircraft although I was buffeted by the concussions. To this day I wonder what would have happened if I had panicked and turned left or right.

Shortly after the above close calls, I asked for and was given a five day leave. Mary Jane met me in Hawaii again. This time we decided to visit the island of Kauai. We spent four wonderful days at the Hanalei Plantation, a remote resort made famous by being the location of the filming of the movie South Pacific. An Elvis Presley movie and several others were also filmed there. In 1996 we went back and retraced our steps of almost thirty years earlier only to find the beautiful old plantation shut down and boarded up. It had been retired and replaced by a huge, sprawling, modern resort about a mile away. We left in disgust.

My leave was over in a blink and I was back in the war. Not long after I returned I got the word that I had been selected for promotion to Major. Captain Bob Matlick, our NETT Operations Officer, was also selected. We had not expected this because neither of us was in the 'Primary Zone' of consideration. Each year the Army selects about five percent of the officers it will promote that year from 'below the zone.' That has the effect of moving the officers selected in front of a whole year group for promotion. It was a great honor and Bob and I received congratulations from all around.

Bob was a great artist. He designed our NETT pocket patch and was especially good at drawing cartoons about day to day events. He would post one on his bulletin board daily and everybody would stop by for a good laugh, sometimes at their own expense. Bob also perfected the technique of erasing clothing off of pictures of women in the newspaper, and drawing in new apparel (and other things). These were also items of much interest on our bulletin board.

Later while a student at Fort Leavenworth, Bob drew and published a book of cartoons about people and events that took place during his year there. His most famous cartoon showed a rear view of two students standing side by side using urinals in the men's room. One was a woman. I don't remember the punch line but it probably had something to do with the increasing number of women then entering the Army. The last time I was at Fort Leavenworth the book was still for sale in the bookstore. Unfortunately, Bob died of a heart attack a few years later while still in the Army. He had been promoted to Colonel and had a promising career ahead.

At this time we were teaching our students the 'wing over' technique of target attack. As I described earlier, every time we performed the maneuver we rolled the aircraft past ninety degrees of bank, or slightly upside down. This caused the gyroscope in our attitude indicator to disengage and become inoperable for up to ten minutes. As long as we had good visibility during the pullout, this was not a problem. But if there were clouds around or we were operating at night, the attitude indicator became absolutely critical.

Our complaint got back to the Bell engineers who selected a replacement indicator that would remain operational in all attitudes. In order to test it Bell requested that a NETT pilot travel back to their plant in Texas. The wanted him to put the new device through the same maneuvers being performed in Vietnam to confirm its adequacy as a good fix. Since I had left my family near the Bell Plant, Major Jarrett thankfully selected me for this dreaded mission. I got another visit with my wife and a few days with my children.

After this mission was completed, and on the way back to the war, I was routed through California to look at a new experimental armed helicopter that was being developed as follow-on to the Cobra. It was called the AH-56 Cheyenne, and it was huge. It had a single main rotor blade for lift and two rotors on its rear, one to counter torque and one to accelerate or slow the aircraft. It looked like something out of a science fiction movie. I did not get to fly it but felt I would get to do so after completing my tour in Vietnam. Once again, as I will relate later, I was wrong.

The Bell engineers had sent me back to Vietnam with one of the new attitude indicators in my briefcase. Soon after my arrival the maintenance platoon installed it in one of our aircraft and a test flight was scheduled for the next morning. That night the airfield came under a rocket attack. You guessed it. The only aircraft hit was the one with the new indicator in it. In a few weeks we received a shipment of indicators and the problem was finally solved.

Near the end of my tour one of our instructor pilots, Chief Warrant Officer Mike Davis was wounded by friendly fire. He had been riding a motorcycle at night and somehow drove at a high rate of speed through a Vietnamese Police checkpoint. Not knowing he was an American, the guards shot Mike in the leg. He was evacuated and later medically retired from the Army. Mike was the only serious casualty among our team members during the entire year.

One sad event that I witnessed was the death of an U.S. Air Force F-100 fighter pilot on his last mission in Vietnam. It was standard at the time for Air Force pilots to complete their tour when they had flown one hundred combat missions. It was also standard that upon return to the airbase from that last mission, the pilot would fly low over the runway and do a barrel roll, then pull up and circle to land. After taxiing in, he would be met by all of the members of his unit, who would douse him with a bottle of champagne, then continue the celebration at the Officer's Club. This particular pilot's aircraft got half way through its roll when a wing came off. He crashed into some bunkers on the airfield parameter, and was killed instantly. There was no celebration this day.

28 August 1967 was the day I completed my second Vietnam tour and departed. That morning I got up, packed my suitcase, checked off the last day on my short-timers calendar, got in a Jeep and had someone drive me to the reporting point. I felt like I was moving in slow motion through a dream. I boarded the aircraft with a quiet and subdued group of mostly ground troops who had been lucky enough to have survived. As on the previous tour, a loud cheer went up when our wheels left the ground. The flight attendants served everyone a free beer, and by the time we were out over the ocean almost everyone on the aircraft was asleep. As at the end of my first tour, I drifted off to sleep sure that I had seen the last of Vietnam.

Original AH-1G Cobra New Equipment Training Team just before deployment to Vietnam in 1967. From left Pratt (armament), Stein (maintenance), me (executive officer), Lee, Hunt, Thomson, Anderson (commander), Matlick (operations), McCarty (supply), Davis, Simpson, Atkinson and in insert Jarrett (deputy commander). All except the commander actively flew as instructor pilots.

CHAPTER 12

BETWEEN TOURS AGAIN

At Travis Air Force Base I changed into civilian clothes for the remainder of my trip home. Returning from my first tour I had been required to travel in uniform. This changed because of the war protesters. I managed to pass through San Francisco Airport early in the morning so saw little of the protests. I flew directly to Nashville and was met by Mary Jane and in spite of feeling somewhat sick, I had another joyous reunion with my family. Over the next several days the tension and apprehension slowly drained out of me and I regained my health.

I had earlier received orders to attend fixed wing transition training at Fort Stewart, Georgia and then multi-engine transition at Fort Rucker, Alabama. Following that, I was to be assigned to Hunter Army Airfield, Georgia, where I would be a Cobra Instructor Pilot. Hunter was the location of the Army's Cobra training school.

Upon reporting to Fort Stewart I was ushered into a Colonel's office. He told me that I had been promoted to Major and pinned the rank on me. I immediately went to the Post Exchange and bought my first field grade hat with the scrambled eggs on the bill. I took it home, put it on and looked at myself in the mirror. With only six plus years of Service, I was looking at one of the youngest Majors in the Army. I was to find out soon that being promoted early meant I could pretty much pick my job assignments.

I completed all of my training without incident and reported for duty. I asked for and was given a staff job in the office of the Director of Instruction at Hunter. The obvious job for me would have been as an instructor pilot, but I had been told that the best career development job was the one that I asked for and got. I was assigned the task of planning for the training of pilots in the new Cheyenne when it arrived. I worked on the plan for a year and shortly after it was completed, the Army cancelled the entire Cheyenne program. They decided that the aircraft was too big, too slow and too expensive for their needs. I had wasted a year on the project but had gained valuable experience that would serve me well later in the Pentagon.

I was reassigned as the staff officer in charge of flight training facilities, a job that I held until my departure a year later. I was in charge of about twelve people who coordinated the maintenance and repair of the School's training airfields. While in that job I frequently flew a T-42 twin engine fixed wing aircraft. It was a welcome change from helicopters.

The T-42 is a four seat military training and administrative flight aircraft.

I had one narrow escape while flying the T-42. I transported my boss to his home in Florida on New Years Day 1970. After dropping him off I flew home by myself. The flight plan carried me directly over Jacksonville, Florida. It was a beautiful day and as I looked down, I could see the Gator Bowl Football Stadium and the game was underway. I wanted to get home in time to see the second half so I expedited my approach into Hunter airfield. I descended too low on my base leg and as I made the ninety degree turn onto final, my wing dipped within what must have been inches of the ground. I had been used to turning a helicopter with the rotors overhead. The T-42 was a low wing design and I had failed to account for the length of the wing. After I got on the ground I realized how close to disaster I had been. I thought about that approach during every fixed wing landing I made for the rest of my flying years.

Shortly after my arrival at Hunter I learned that Georgia Southern University was conducting a Masters of Business Administration (MBA) night school program on the base. I immediately signed up. For two years I worked my normal job during the day, spent nights in the classroom, and weekends writing research papers. I do not remember much about the tour because I was so busy. It paid off because I was selected in my first year of eligibility for Command and General Staff College, a full year graduate level school at Fort Leavenworth, Kansas.

Mary Jane was pregnant with Tom. In order to complete our travel before her approaching due date, we were allowed to move to Kansas early. I was given the job of teaching all of the incoming pilots how to fly the T-41, a single engine fixed wing training aircraft. I had a lot of fun and got to know all of the aviators in the class. The only bad part was trying to teach some Navy pilots how to fly the aircraft. They had been flying much larger aircraft and tried to land about fifty feet above the runway. I had to take the controls and salvage several landings.

My year at Fort Leavenworth was very rewarding because of the lifelong friends I made. I was part of a group of very junior officers who lived in leased houses in Kansas City, Kansas and commuted about twenty five miles to school. There were about twelve families on the street and we became very close. Many of the officers eventually reached General Officer rank. Two of them attained four star ranks and one became Chief of Staff of the Army.

After Leavenworth I was assigned to the 1st Infantry Division at Fort Riley, Kansas. I requested to go to the Division Artillery for a ground (non-flying) assignment. I was initially assigned as the assistant S3 (operations officer). After about a month the S3 (a Lieutenant Colonel) departed so I got his job. I kept it several months during which the Division deployed to Germany for a large field training exercise (known as Reforger). It was a great experience to maneuver and control several artillery battalions in the biggest of all annual field exercises.

Upon return from Europe, I got the assignment I had been fighting for: battalion operations officer (S3). I was assigned to the 1st Battalion,

7th Field Artillery. The former battalion commander had recently been relieved from his job, and the unit was in bad shape. A new commander, Lieutenant Colonel Don Whalen, took over the unit. He wanted a staff college graduate to help him get the battalion back on track, so he selected me over several other candidates. At that time it was very unusual for an aviator with no field artillery experience to get an S3 job. I loved it, and under LTC Whalen's leadership, I prospered.

I spent the entire winter of 1971-72 living in a tent in the field at Fort Riley. I scheduled each firing battery to spend one week a month in the field. I took a small evaluation team out with them to supervise their training. With three batteries, that meant that I had to spend three weeks of every month in the field. This lasted for four months. By the time spring came we were trained better than any other artillery battalion in the Division Artillery. We won the annual spring gunnery competition 'hands down.'

About seven months into this job, and while out in the field, I got a radio message to call my branch assignment officer in Washington. A cold chill went down my spine. I knew this could not be good news. On the long drive back to our headquarters I contemplated the possibility of a third Vietnam tour for the first time.

Sure enough, I was told that because of the Spring, 1972 North Vietnamese offensive, I was being ordered back to Vietnam to take command a Cobra Aerial Rocket Artillery Battery. My immediate challenge was figuring out how to give Mary Jane the bad news. There was no way to sugar coat it, so I just went home and told her.

I figured that she would feel sorry for me but her immediate reaction was: "Oh no! What will I do with Tom." He was then two years old and a terror to keep up with. A few days earlier he had climbed out of a ground floor window and fell on his head (no injury). About the same time he wandered away from home and to our horror, was found by my commander and brought back to the house. We decided immediately that Mary Jane and the family would have to move to Tennessee close to family where she could get help with the children.

At Fort Riley we lived on base in a duplex with an unusual neighbor. He was a medical doctor at the base hospital, was a draftee, and was against the Vietnam War. When he found out that I was going back to Vietnam for a third time, he took pity on my family and asked what he could do to help. We told him the family would not be living near an Army medical facility, so he decided to provide Mary Jane with a 'care package' of medicine. He wrote prescriptions for all of the medicine he thought she and the children might need to survive my absence. He delivered a shoe box full which met the family's needs for the entire year.

CHAPTER 13

FINAL COMBAT TOUR

After settling the family in Cookeville Tennessee, and with a heavy heart, I climbed aboard a commercial airliner for another trip to Vietnam. I flew into the Saigon airport on about 20 June 1972. The approach and landing was different than anything I had experienced before. The North Vietnamese had introduced heat seeking anti aircraft missiles into the war. To minimize the danger from these weapons, passenger flights into Saigon were made at night. We flew over the airport at about ten thousand feet. The pilot depressurized the aircraft, cut the engines and went into a rapid circling descent. We landed safely but I had a bad feeling. In 1964 civilian aircraft operated freely around the airfield and our helicopters were parked in the open along the runway. In 1967 we had to contend with frequent rocket attacks and our aircraft were parked in bunkers. Now we had to worry about air defense missiles. I had seen it go from one extreme to the other, and knew we were not winning the War.

For a few days I remained in Saigon while the personnel officer decided where to send me. The Cobra battery that I had been told I was to command had been deactivated, and sent home. During the weeks it took for me to get from Fort Riley to Vietnam, the President had decided to stop all offensive ground combat operations, and the units were being rapidly deactivated.

I was assigned to command the 18th Corps Aviation Company (CAC). It was located in Can Tho, about one hundred miles south of Saigon. The unit's mission was to provide aviation support to all of the American forces in the southern third of the country during the withdrawal phase of the war. For the first time in my Vietnam experience, I was assigned to a 'slick' unit and not a 'gun' unit.

The 18th CAC consisted of about forty five aircraft and over three hundred men, about twice the size of a standard aviation company. It

Major Douglas Thorpe (left) hands me command of the 18th Aviation Company on 26 June, 1972. Looking on is Lieutenant Colonel William Benton Jr. the 164th Aviation Group Commander

Company crest and crew chief's name was painted on our Huey's radio compartment covers. This one was configured for a senior commander with an extra radio antenna mounted on the skids.

had a platoon of twelve CH-47 Chinook helicopters (radio call sign 'Hill Climber'), a platoon of twelve OH-58 Kiowa helicopters (radio call sign 'Bartender'), and two platoons of ten UH-1H Iroquois each (radio call sign 'Green Delta'). It also had a maintenance platoon, a headquarters platoon and an airfield security platoon.

At this point in the war all of the U.S. infantry and artillery forces had been withdrawn from Vietnam. The country was divided into four Corps areas and each of these areas subdivided into Provinces. Each Province had a Vietnamese Army unit stationed in it, and the commander of that unit was usually also the Province Chief. The U.S. Army had a small team (ten to twenty men) located in each Province to coordinate American helicopter support and advise on tactical matters. There were sixteen Provinces in the Corps area that my unit supported.

On my first two tours in Vietnam my missions were categorized as 'combat missions.' The 18th CAC missions were categorized as 'combat support missions.' They were generated daily by the advisory teams in each Province. We usually sent at least one helicopter to each Province each day. These aircraft transported and distributed supplies, mail and people to outposts throughout the Province. They also conducted road and area reconnaissance missions, but usually stayed above one thousand feet because they flew alone and were unarmed except for two door mounted machine guns. If they found something suspicious they did not try to engage, but reported it to the Vietnamese who had artillery, air and infantry forces with which to respond.

I arrived at Can Tho airfield on 25 June 1972, and took command the next day. The departing commander, Major Douglas Thorpe, had organized the unit in 1971 from the assets of departing units as they stood down. We only had a few hours of overlap because he departed immediately after the change of command. I felt confident about my capabilities, and had no trouble getting in the saddle.

At that time there were two aviation units located on the airfield: the 18th CAC (my company) and C Troop of the 16th Air Cavalry. The Cavalry lived on the south side of the runway and my unit owned the north side. Air cavalry troops conducted themselves with the swagger and confidence of the gunship pilots that I had been so much a part of on my previous two tours. They saw themselves superior to my 'slick' pilots. To put it mildly, the two groups did not mix well. They would sometimes argue and fight in the officers clubs after duty hours. When the word got out that a gunship pilot with two tours already under his belt had taken command of the 18th CAC, the friction decreased.

My first big challenge had nothing to do with my new job, but my living quarters. The unit's officers lived in one story wooden buildings that contained eight rooms per building, four on one side back-to-back with four on the other. Doug had taken me into his room, which was to become mine. It was about fourteen feet long by about twelve feet wide with a single bed, dresser, desk and two chairs. As I looked it over Doug said that this was not really going to be my room. He pushed a wall panel and opened a hidden door that led into the room behind the one we were in. I was flabbergasted.

Doug explained that all commanders on the airbase lived in fear for their lives at the hands of their own soldiers! A grim process known as 'fragging' had been ongoing for several months in Vietnam, mostly in infantry units. Disgruntled soldiers who had disagreements with a commander would first warn him by throwing a smoke grenade in his sleeping quarters. If the problems were not resolved within a few days, the soldier would next toss a tear gas grenade. If that failed to get results, a fragmentation grenade was thrown, which often killed the commander.

Fragging had evolved because of a multitude of problems then existing in the Army. There was a low state of morale among the draftee soldiers. In addition there was widespread use of illegal drugs. I had heard vague rumors about fragging before my arrival, but was really surprised to hear that it was a potential problem in aviation units.

I spent one night in the hidden room. The next day the airfield commander contacted me and offered me a small house trailer inside a guarded compound in a corner of the airbase. This facility had been built for senior officers but most of them had departed as units stood down. I decided to make the move, thus separating myself from the day to day living environment of the remainder of the unit. In keeping with the hidden sleeping area idea, I set up a bedroom in one end of the trailer and left the curtains open so it was visible, but slept in the other end.

Fortunately, I was never threatened with fragging. I cannot say the same for my boss. He got a smoke grenade thrown into his trailer and a few nights later, a tear gas grenade arrived. However, he was forewarned about the second one and managed to catch the grenade thrower and put him in jail for a long time. After that, there were no more fragging attempts at Can Tho.

After getting settled into my quarters I concentrated on learning something about the unit and its people. My senior NCO, First Sergeant R.A. Jones, took me on a tour of our facilities. The enlisted soldiers lived in two story barracks buildings. Each building had a bunker located nearby that provided some protection from mortar and rocket attacks. As the First Sergeant led me through a bunker I noticed several small white and blue bottles about the size of sewing thimbles lying on the floor. He explained that these were the containers in which illegal drugs were purchased. Each had contained a dose of pure heroin that had been bought for about five Dollars, and inhaled through the nose by a soldier. Sergeant Jones picked up the bottles, and upon return to his office, added them to a huge stack with plastic glue. I knew right then that I was going to have to confront a serious drug problem.

An illustration of the drug problem I inherited when I took command. Pictured are hundreds of little five Dollar illegal heroin bottles that were collected by the First Sergeant and glued together to prevent reuse.

To confront this problem I immediately changed drug testing from once a month to once a week. I informed the chain of command that there was no room in my unit for anyone who even thought about taking drugs. I did some research and found out that as a field grade commanding officer, I could with no questions asked, ship any soldier that came up positive on a drug test to a holding unit in Saigon. There he would be held behind bars until he could be shipped to a rehabilitation station back in the States. This procedure had been instituted to reduce fragging, and it worked.

My intent was to strike terror in the minds of drug users and potential drug users. I developed a procedure by which I would personally get a call from the unit that conducted the frequent drug tests. They provided me with the names of soldiers who tested positive. As soon as I got the call I contacted flight operations and told them to move a helicopter to the 'hot spot' (landing pad close to my headquarters), and keep it running.

I would then tell the First Sergeant to go get the positive soldier at his job and take him directly to the waiting helicopter. He got no notice, no opportunity to go back to his room, no collection of possessions and no chance to say good-by to buddies. He got no opportunity to collect or pay debts, and no chance to say farewell to any girl friends. Most importantly, he got no recourse, no chance to make excuses and no time to think about fragging. He simply disappeared from the unit. He was flown directly to Saigon and within an hour was in detention. Two days later he was in a drug rehabilitation center in California.

After a few of these disappearances the word got out, and the incidence of positive drug tests declined, then ceased. These tests were for hard drugs so I still had to deal with marijuana smoking. I did that by walking through the barracks and bunkers at odd times, usually at night, and with some big Sergeants. I simply sniffed out the users. Marijuana has a distinctive odor and was easy to detect. Those that I caught suffered the same fate as the hard drug users. One night I caught my senior aircraft mechanic, a Specialist Seven, puffing a weed. I ended his career. His departure demonstrated that I had no pity on drug abusers, no matter who they were. From that time forward drug problems in the unit were insignificant.

Simultaneously with solving the drug problem I flew missions every day. I would fly as copilot with a randomly selected crew in their aircraft. I flew to each of the sixteen Provinces in turn, and participated in the regularly scheduled support mission for the day. In each Province I met with the Senior advisor to solicit his ideas and suggestions on how we could improve our support of his mission. During this period I got to know my pilots and crews, became familiar with our Corps area, and established a relationship with our customers, the advisory teams. Upon completion of this effort I wrote a report that found its way to my senior aviation boss. It was well received and instrumental in establishing my credibility as a competent commander. That paid great dividends later on when I started losing crews and needed chain of command support.

Sometime in December 1972, I was bitten by a rabid dog. I had gone with the First Sergeant to break open a locked room that held the belongings of a soldier that had gone away without leave (AWOL). Noises had been heard coming from the room so we went to investigate. The lock was cut and the door swung open. Out jumped a small brown dog. Before we could do anything to restrain him he took a big bite out of my leg. He was captured and sent to the Veterinarian for evaluation.

The test results came back positive for rabies. I was immediately started on a series of five rabies shots, one every other day. By that time in my life the Army had given me hundreds of shots and vaccinations, but nothing that compared to the rabies series. They were given with a large needle and shot into the muscles around and in front of the stomach. Each caused a huge blue lump. By the time I had taken the last one, my stomach was so sore I could not bend over. I looked like I had been shot with a shot gun. Since that time I have always given stray dogs the right of way.

The company had a recurring classified mission. We would paint over all of the U.S. Army markings on a Huey, dress in civilian clothing, leave all of our personal identity behind, and fly up the Mekong River to Phnom Pen, Cambodia. We would spend the day there and fly support missions for the American Embassy and the Cambodian Army. Our politicians were at that time telling the international community and the American public that we were not operating outside of Vietnam.

I decided to fly one of these missions. We took off from Can Tho and flew up the river for about two hours. Upon arrival over Phnom Pen Airport, we talked in English to the tower and were directed to park in an isolated area. As we landed I saw several old Soviet fighter aircraft sitting around. I knew I was in a strange and hostile place.

We flew a few short missions for the American Embassy, then departed for our return flight. We were transporting a Cambodian General and some of his staff to Vietnam for a meeting. About halfway back to Can Tho the helicopter suddenly started to vibrate up and down violently. Because of my test pilot experience I was able to immediately isolate it as a main rotor control problem. One of the blades was going in and out of track as it rotated (the blades must follow each other exactly for the ride to be smooth). I was immediately wet with sweat. I knew it was a serious and potentially deadly problem. I got my copilot on the radio with our unit to report our situation (thank goodness we were at the relatively high altitude of three thousand feet), and began to experiment, trying to find control inputs that would reduce the vibration.

I was tempted to turn the power off and descend as rapidly as possible. There were problems with that. We were over solid triple canopy jungle. There was no place to land and as always, we were without parachutes. When I made any attempt to reduce power, the vibration increased. I then noticed that by slightly increasing power, the vibration would almost go away. However, this didn't solve the problem because with increased power we would climb higher, and I knew that at some point we would be forced to come back down.

By now the Cambodian General knew something was badly wrong. He was making low moaning noises that I could hear through my flight helmet. I wanted to get him on the ground safely, but I wanted to get my crew down even more. About the only thing I had left to try was to roll off the throttle, thereby reducing power without reducing the pitch in the blades. Miraculously this seemed to work. With lower rotor RPM we started a decent of about one hundred feet per minute. At that rate it would take us thirty minutes to get to the ground. As it turned out, about thirty minutes down the river we crossed into Vietnam at a friendly outpost. When we got there my skills were tested as I flew the aircraft onto the ground with forward airspeed (known as a running landing).

With the rotor system unloaded, I killed the engine and the rotors jarringly stopped turning. I thought the Cambodians were going to kiss the ground. They jumped out and disappeared, probably to never fly again. My copilot made a report to our unit which had already launched a couple of aircraft in our direction. They were happy to receive the news that we were safely on the ground. I was picked up and taken back to the unit while maintenance personnel put a new part on my aircraft and flew it back.

The mechanic found that a bearing connecting two rotating components had failed and was completely gone. The arm that adjusted the pitch of one of the blades was flapping up and down. The malfunctioning components resembled a bolt the size of a cigar bouncing around inside a hole the size of a coffee cup. If I had taken the obvious corrective action that most pilots would have taken, and completely reduced the pitch of the blades, the rotor head would have disintegrated. I had somehow cheated death again.

Shortly afterwards, C troop 16th Air Cavalry, the other unit on Can Tho Airfield, had a deadly accident on their aircraft parking ramp. C Troop flew a small observation helicopter, the OH-6 Cayuse. During their reconnaissance missions they would sometimes hover over a suspected enemy fighting position or 'spider hole,' and toss a hand grenade into it.

This occasionally resulted in the helicopter getting hit by the crew's own grenade shrapnel. One of their smart guys decided to fix this by making some delay action bombs. He found that by pulling the safety pin out of a hand grenade and placing it into a half quart glass container, he could create a handy bomb. When the thing was thrown the glass would break on impact and release the safety spoon on the grenade. A few seconds later, and when the helicopter was a safe distance away, the grenade would detonate.

This worked fine until a crew chief accidentally dropped a box of bombs as they were being loaded into his helicopter for a mission. One or more of the bottles broke and before the crew could react, the whole box detonated, causing the aircraft to explode killing the crewman. There was nothing left but a big black spot in the parking space. Here was another example of needless death among our forces in Vietnam.

The first aircraft I lost while in command took place on 28 October 1972. My best OH-58 Kiowa pilot, Chief Warrant Officer Mitchell Stever, crashed his aircraft into a river south of Can Tho. It was standard procedure at that time to fly the small OH-58 without a copilot or door gunner, thus making all of the seats available to the supported units. Mitchell had just completed his mission and had dropped an American advisor off on a small helicopter pad next to a river. The pad was surrounded with waist high rolls of barbed wire. Preparing to depart, he was the only person in the aircraft. That made the aircraft a bit tail heavy. Without looking behind himself, he brought the aircraft to a hover and started backing away from the landing pad, intending to hover out over the water, turn the nose into the wind, and take off.

The tail of his aircraft was lower than he thought. The tail skid, a two feet long steel rod that extended down and back at an angle from the rear of the tail boom, caught the top strand of barbed wire. As the aircraft continued backward, the wire gave some, then pulled tight. The helicopter's nose started to come up. Thinking that he was encountering a gust of wind, Mitchell pulled in maximum power and the helicopter did a complete back flip and landed in the river upside down.

The advisor who had just departed the aircraft watched all of this. He immediately jumped into the river and swam to the aircraft, pulling Mitchell to safety. Unfortunately, when the rotor blades hit the water, one had broken and slammed into the cockpit, causing severe injury to Mitchell's chest. A CH-47 that was operating nearby picked him up and flew him directly to the hospital in Saigon. He lived for a few days and died of complications from infections picked up in the filthy water of the river.

We flew with all of the doors off of our OH-58 Kiowas. The pilot and copilot had armored seats. At the far right you can see the little tail skid. One like it cost Warrant Officer Stever his life

I arrived at the crash site after Mitchell had been evacuated and in time to watch the aircraft being lifted out of the water by one of my Hueys. Standing there, I smoked the first cigarette I had tried in over four years. Three days later I would smoke again when I lost another aircraft.

In early October 1972 the platoon leader of my CH-47 platoon completed his tour. I selected a fine young Captain named Steven D. Howard to replace him. A couple of weeks later one of his pilots (I do not remember the pilots name but he was a Lieutenant), had a mission to fly from Can Tho to Saigon and back. It was the pilot's birthday. Captain Howard met the Lieutenant when he came out to preflight the aircraft and awarded him the day off. Steven took the Lieutenant's place as one of the pilots for the mission. Late that afternoon, while flying at about three thousand feet and on their way back from Saigon, an enemy SA-7 heat seeking guided missile hit one of their engines and blew it off, taking the aft rotor system with it. The aircraft went into what was reported to be a dive of more than forty five degrees and crashed killing all aboard.

The first I knew of the crash was when I met the birthday Lieutenant coming out of Flight Operations crying and saying it should have been him. I flew to the crash site but could not land or see anything because of a heavy thunderstorm. I found out by radio that a patrol of Vietnamese soldiers had reached the crash site, secured it, and found no survivors. It took several days to dig out all of the remains due to the depth the aircraft penetrated into the rice paddy. There were thirteen soldiers on board. All but one was from my company. My radio repair section, which had been to Saigon for a day off, was particularly hard hit.

I wrote twelve letters to the next of kin and we conducted a memorial ceremony in our little chapel. In keeping with tradition, there were twelve pairs of empty boots lined up across the front of the room. As tough as it was, we had to go back to work the next day.

In 1972 all Army UH-1 Hueys in Vietnam were equipped with a device attached to the tailpipe to deflect hot exhaust gases upward. Known as the 'Bell Scoop,' it prevented a heat seeking SA-7 missile from locking on and guiding to the aircraft. However, our CH-47s had no such protection. Therefore, we decided to ground the platoon until we could install something to protect the aircraft from the missile threat.

The Army rushed U.S. Air Force flare dispensers to us, which were immediately installed on the rear ramps of the big aircraft. These dispensers were similar to the smoke dispensers we had installed on our Cobras in 1968. They consisted of a box of about forty eight small flares that could be launched out behind the aircraft. A crewmember was required to lay on the lowered rear cargo ramp with a switch in his

Our CH-47 Chinooks were backed into U shaped bunkers to minimize vulnerability to enemy mortars.

hand. He was secured to the aircraft with a rope tether (called a 'monkey rope'). Upon observing the smoke trail of a missile coming off of the ground, he would punch out some flares. They would ignite just behind the aircraft and, in theory, present a heat source hotter than the engine exhaust. Hopefully, the SA-7 would home on the flares, allowing the aircraft to escape out of range.

We did not know if the flares would work. Predictably, the flight crews were nervous about resuming flight operations with an untested device. Therefore, to reassure them, I decided to fly with them on the first mission going back into the area where we had lost the aircraft. As we passed near the crash site the Flight Engineer on the ramp, SP5 James L Scroggins, reported seeing a missile launch behind us. He immediately started deploying flares.

I was riding in the cockpit between and behind the pilot and copilot. As I looked back out of the open rear end of the aircraft, I saw the flares being fired and suddenly, just behind the aircraft, I saw an explosion. The missile had apparently impacted a flare. We nervously continued our mission and upon return to base, I reported the event up the chain of command. The next day the First Aviation Brigade Commander, Brigadier General Jack Mackmull, came to Can Tho and pinned a Distinguished Flying Cross on James, crediting him with saving the aircraft and all on board. I was told later that this was the first documented account of a flare saving an Army helicopter. Unfortunately, James was killed in a later shoot-down.

During these final months of my tour I could call Mary Jane by simply dialing direct from my desk. The call went through instantly on a satellite. This contrasted vividly with the telephone system in 1964.

When I called home at that time the call had to go by radio to the Philippines, then under the ocean by wire through Hawaii to the West Coast, and then processed as a long distance call to Tennessee. That earlier call had taken hours to put through, and we had to say 'over' at the end of each transmission.

In December my branch assignment officer called to inform me that I would be assigned to the Office of the Director of Army Aviation in the Pentagon when I returned. That was good news because I wanted to serve on the Army Staff. I called home to give Mary Jane the news and we started planning our move to Washington, D.C.

My desk was a busy place just before the Company departed in March, 1973. All aircraft, equipment, supplies, facilities and people had to be disposed of in an orderly and accountable manner.

At our 1972-73 New Years Eve party each of my Officers (over 100) poured a container of adult beverage over my head at the stroke of midnight. I almost froze to death. It took a whole day to clean up the mess.

During January of 1973 we watched closely as the Paris peace talks went into their final stages. Finally, we were told that at 5:30 AM on 29 January 1973 the cease-fire would take effect. Until that time we would continue to be fair game for rocket and mortar attacks. In fact, intelligence reported that the North Vietnamese planned one last attack just minutes before the cease fire became effective.

I ordered the entire unit to be inside of bunkers starting an hour before the magic moment. A couple of minutes before the appointed hour the base siren sounded. Suddenly there was a big boom. A mortar round had landed harmlessly nearby. We assumed this was the start of a big attack, but as it turned out, that was the only round fired. The 'all clear' signal was sounded and we went back to work.

Our final mission as a unit was to prepare to take off immediately after the cease-fire and pick up released American and Vietnamese prisoners of war. The unit had not been training for formation flying so getting up to speed for that became a priority. We flew several training missions, practicing takeoffs and landings in small then large groups. This mission was never executed because all of the American prisoners had been moved to Hanoi, and the Vietnamese prisoners that were released in our area were picked up by the Vietnamese Air Force.

On the first day of the cease-fire we did fly several missions to pick up American advisors from the Provinces. We were told to take our machine guns off of the aircraft, and carry only personal side arms. On one of the flights one of my aircraft was on its way back to Can Tho with a load of advisors when it was hit several times with enemy small arms fire. The copilot, Warrant Officer Anthony Dal Pozzo, Jr. was hit in thc head and killed. Some of the advisors were wounded.

Obviously, the North Vietnamese soldiers were not honoring the cease-fire. We had accepted the orders from our chain of command to disarm and had lost one of our own for our effort. That night my pilots got together and decided they did not want to fly any more without some way to protect themselves. I reported the incident to higher headquarters and requested permission to carry larger weapons, but got no help. I decided on my own to designate the fully automatic M-16 rifle as the personal sidearm of all crewmembers. From that date till we stood down, we carried M-16s in plain sight in each door on all flights. Nobody ever said anything.

During February and March we were often required to transport Vietcong and North Vietnamese members of the Joint Military Commission (JMC), which had been created by the cease-fire agreement. It was empowered to supervise the execution of the cease-fire, and was composed of members from the four combatants: the two named above and the U.S. Military and the South Vietnamese Military. My flight crews had great fun at the bar each night as they told of their efforts to harass their former enemies. Ninety degree banks during turns and sudden power off landings were very successful in making the North Vietnamese airsick. Of course, I officially knew nothing about it.

Another organization, the International Control Commission was also created. Its mission was to perform the function of referee during the execution of the peace deal. It was composed of members from Poland, Canada and two other countries that I do not remember. My unit also supported this group with helicopters.

Flight Engineer Scroggins, whose flares had saved my life earlier in a CH-47, was killed in February 1973. He was a crewmember on another CH-47 that was shot down, this time by small arms fire. He was badly burned in the resulting crash which occurred on 17 February, and died a few days later on 23 February. The sad part of it was that this mission took place well after the cease-fire.

His Chinook was supporting the JMC by delivering cargo near Song Be. The material was to be used to construct latrine facilities among other things. After the aircraft made the drop off, and while climbing through about five hundred feet of altitude over a highway, a North Vietnamese unit opened up with numerous AK-47s. Several hits were scored on the helicopter, setting it on fire. It crashed intact on a road but was quickly consumed by flames. The injured crew was picked up by a passing Huey and flown to a hospital. All but Specialist Five Scroggins survived. He was the last American aviation crewmember to die in Vietnam before the final combat troop withdrawal that occurred on 28 March 1973.

As we prepared to depart I was asked to seek volunteers from among pilots and crewmembers to stay behind after March 28th and fly the Peace Commission aircraft. From my notebook where I kept notes during that tour (the only tour during which I kept notes), I recorded the criteria given the potential volunteers: "personnel: all must be volunteers; purpose is MIA and POW rescue; flight time to expect: three hours per day six days per week with Sunday off; expect fifty five to seventy five flight hours per month; Crews: two pilots and two crewmembers per flight.' Needless to say, almost every pilot that was left in the unit tried to volunteer. Only about twelve were selected.

In early February 1973 we got serious about standing down. We had been instructed to phase down flight operations gradually until they completely stopped in early March, and to plan to leave all of our equipment except the CH-47s and the OH-58s behind for the Vietnamese Air Force. The Vietnamese did not have these two types of aircraft, so we shipped them back to the United Stated. I would see the CH-47s again in about two years as part of the battalion I would command.

We were told to strip everything but military furniture out of our living quarters. This presented a problem for the enlisted barracks because over the years the soldiers had scrounged all kinds of lumber and other junk to turn the open bay building into small private rooms. It all had to be torn out and disposed of. First Sergeant J. A. White, who had replaced First Sergeant R. A. Jones, assigned a detail of soldiers to rip out everything and load it onto trucks. The junk was then transported to a huge sandbagged area about the size of a basketball court, and dumped in a pile. He then allowed the Vietnamese employees that worked on the base to have whatever they wanted. The pile soon disappeared.

My top NCO during the stand-down, First Sergeant White, holds our Company Guide-on. We are wearing company and 164th Group patches on our pockets and green combat leadership tabs on our shoulders.

An interesting item that we had to turn over for shipment back home was our 'Blood Chit.' It was a piece of cloth with an American Flag printed on it. Below the flag in fourteen different languages was an offer of a reward for the safe return of the downed American airman. Our chits were considered sensitive items. They were accounted for by serial number just like weapons, and we carried them on all missions. One day my Supply Sergeant came in and asked me if I wanted one as a souvenir. I took it and today it is one of my most prized memorabilia. I never asked how the Sergeant got the chit off of the books, but I suspect he reported it lost in combat.

As we frantically prepared to depart there were thousands of administrative details that had to be taken care of. Efficiency reports and awards had to be written. The headquarters in Saigon had given me authority to approve awarding the Commendation Medal, the Bronze

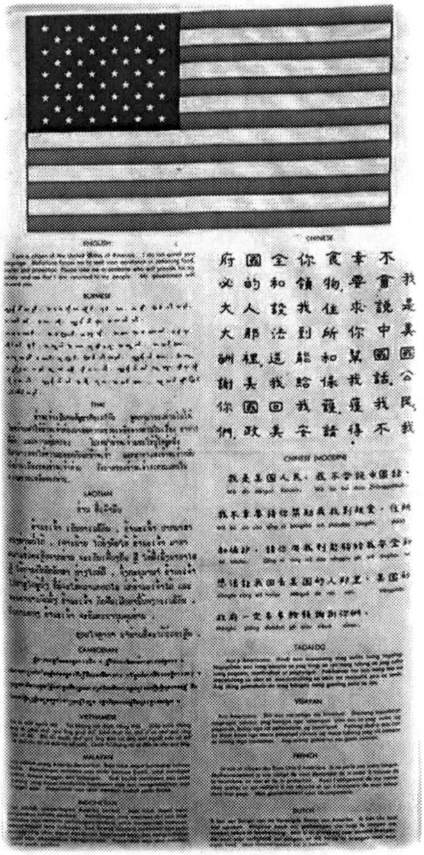

The Blood Chit says in 14 languages:

"I am a citizen of the United States of America. I do not speak your language. Misfortune forces me to seek your assistance in obtaining food, shelter and protection. Please take me to someone who will provide for my safety and see that I am returned to my people. My Government will reward you."

Star Medal and the Air Medal. We had to prepare orders and certificates for each award given.

Award citations were mass produced by subordinate leaders and typed by our clerks. Once we had them completed, we held a huge awards ceremony at which I presented literally hundreds of medals.

I prepared a phase-out plan by platoon, and left it up to the subordinate leaders to pick specific departure dates for their people. Orders were then published and the people proceeded to Saigon on their appointed date, where they boarded aircraft for their flight home. The process went smoothly until late February when all departures were put on hold. That left about seventy five of us with nothing to do but wait.

The Paris Peace Talks with the North Vietnamese being held in Paris had broken down. Therefore, our Government decided to stop U.S. troop withdrawals until all of the POWs were released. In effect, my little group was being held hostage.

Stacked row on row are hundreds of medals that I presented at our final formation. Most were routine awards for service in Vietnam. We called them 'I was there medals'

My crew chief stands with me in front of my aircraft in early 1973. The strap in his hand was used to secure the aircraft doors against sappers when it was on the ground. Reluctantly I left all of the Hueys behind when I departed.

We moved off of the Can Tho airbase and into a compound in the town. The airbase was turned over to the Vietnamese Air Force. We left everything in place: weapons in the weapons room, gas masks in the storage room etc. Most disturbing, we left our thirty Huey Helicopters on the ramp with the maintenance records for each one in its front seat. It was a sad day for me because the aircraft were almost new, well maintained and I knew that the Vietnamese Air Force would soon trash them. I suspect a lot of them ended up in the ocean in 1975 when so many were flown out to our ships to escape the advancing North Vietnamese Army.

On the day we departed Can Tho for Saigon we were told to leave our flight helmets behind for the Vietnamese. I collected about fifty in my Jeep trailer. I still had my Jeep so was able to drive myself to the airfield for our departure. The remainder of my unit followed behind in a bus with our luggage. There I left the ignition key in the vehicle, trailer and all and walked away without looking back. As I stepped from the bright sunlight of the runway into the dark interior of the windowless C-130 transport I felt a huge flush of relief spread over. The burden of command was lifted.

I did have some apprehension as I boarded for the short flight to Saigon. A few days earlier an identical aircraft had crashed on takeoff from an airfield to our south, and a full load of Americans headed home had perished. Our flight went without a hitch, and less than an hour later we joined several hundred other 'hostages' at the holding area in Saigon.

We were held in the old 'Camp Alpha' through which tens of thousands of U.S. soldiers had processed during the war. Upon arrival the members of my unit disappeared into the crowd, and I knew my command tour was over. I sat at a table in the snack bar and reluctantly removed the green tabs of command from my shoulders. It was a memorable moment in my life. I still have the tabs.

For the next several days we had nothing to do but read and sleep. We had no access to television, so did not get to follow the repatriation of our POWs. Once the last ones were safely in the Philippines we boarded a civilian 747 and departed. That took place at about dark on 28 March 1973. As we boarded the aircraft we were counted by a group of four military officers in uniform consisting of one each American, Vietcong, Vietnamese, and North Vietnamese. It was humiliating that after about one thousand days of personal involvement in the war in Vietnam, my last sight on entering the aircraft was that of my enemy in uniform and standing in a place of authority.

For the third time in my life, I experienced the joy of getting out of that country alive. As in the past, a cheer went up as the wheels left the ground. It was dark and as I looked out the window I got my last view of Vietnam. Fittingly, it was of flares hanging on parachutes north of our flight path. I set back, closed my eyes, and tried to reflect back on my experiences in Vietnam. Soon I switched to thinking about getting back to my family and home. We flew to Guam where we were allowed a few minutes off of the aircraft while it was refueled. I just had time to joyfully call home and report my progress, and to go into the Base Exchange and purchase a bottle of liquid refreshment to ease my long flight.

As on earlier tours, we processed through Travis Air Force Base in California and proceeded on our own to our homes. Again I passed through the air terminals in civilian clothing and had the feeling I was sneaking home. For a third time I was reunited with Mary Jane in Nashville and drove home to see my beautiful children. As in the past, I was sick for days as the pressure and pain of the last few months slowly eased.

Following my final return from Vietnam in 1973, I served seventeen more years in the Army. Throughout that period I was filled with sadness that all of my effort and all of my lost friends and comrades went for nothing. I was not bitter at the Army because it was only following orders. I was, however, and remain bitter that our liberal politicians, the American press and a large number of misinformed Americans citizens gave up on our friends in South Vietnam and proceeded to lose the war when the U.S. Military could easily have won it.

CHAPTER 14

THE COLD WAR YEARS

At the end of the Vietnam War the Army was in shambles. Drug use was widespread. Probably the biggest problem was that the Non Commissioned Officer's (NCO) Corps' lower ranks were very weak. These junior leaders had been drafted and most had attained their rank in the permissive environment of Vietnam. They had no idea how to effectively lead peacetime soldiers.

To correct the Vietnam hangover, the government ended the draft and called on the Services to modernize their forces. The aircraft we brought home from Vietnam had been adequate for low intensity warfare. The threat however, was from the Soviet Union in Europe's high intensity battlefield environment. We needed aircraft with more powerful engines, better survivability (ability to take hits and continue to fly), and longer range anti-armor weapons.

In 1973 the Army initiated an all out effort to develop the needed modern equipment and the tactics to support it. As the new systems came on line the relevance of the Cardinal Rules essentially disappeared. A few years later when the Cold War ended and insurgencies moved back to the forefront, they reemerged.

To upgrade the people part of the Army something called the 'Modern Volunteer Army' was introduced. It was designed to attract sufficient volunteers to fill the ranks. We lowered appearance standards, provided more privacy in the barracks, introduced a whole new series of military schools, offered civilian education incentives and accepted women in all but direct combat units.

Over the next several years we found out that soldiers did not want it soft. They wanted to be challenged. In order to provide that challenge we changed the recruiting theme to 'Be all you can be.' Over the years this effort was fine-tuned and eventually produced the Army that so brilliantly won the 1991 Gulf War and the wars in Afghanistan and Iraq. I was fortunate to participate directly in the transition and rebuilding of the Army. I retired in 1990 only one month before Iraq invaded Kuwait. I was able to set back and watch, with much satisfaction, what the Army could accomplish when allowed by the politicians to win. In a small way I had contributed to the Army's post-Vietnam successes.

A few weeks after my return from Vietnam in 1973 I traveled to the Washington, DC area and bought a house in Vienna, Virginia. Sometime in April I reported to my new job in the Pentagon. It was a dream job for a young Major. I was a staff officer in the office that was responsible for preparing and defending before the U.S. Congress the Aviation portion of the U.S. Army Budget. I was involved in giving briefings to, and writing papers for the Army Staff, the Department of Defense and finally, the Appropriations and Armed Services Committees of both the House and Senate.

As mentioned earlier, great change was underway in the Army. We were turning away from Vietnam and starting development of a whole new family of equipment. I worked on a team that was defining performance requirements for the AH-64 Apache, the UH-60 Blackhawk and the tilt rotor aircraft now flying in the U.S. Marine Corps. I was also involved in starting programs that modernized the CH-47 Chinook and the OH-58 Kiowa.

We worked about twelve hours a day and often on weekends. Our weekend work in the Pentagon ceased when General Abrams took over as Chief of Staff of the Army. He put out the word that weekends were for the family. He would walk the halls on Saturday and run off anyone he found in the building. I happened to be one of the first ones he found. I was in civilian clothes so he didn't see my nametag, and didn't get in trouble. I went home and from then on, spent weekends with the family. Like many great ideas, it was not very practical in light of our workload. The job had to get done so I was forced to take the work home and complete it on the kitchen table.

In those days action officers, as we were called, did not do their own typing. In fact, there were no computers in the offices. We had civilian secretaries that did all the typing. They had a machine that used a magnetic tape to record the work as it went onto paper. This machine was capable of printing a draft, then going back and allowing changes to be make before printing a final copy.

I soon discovered that about everything had been written down somewhere earlier. I became an expert at 'cut and paste.' I would string my papers together out of many pieces and staple them into one long scroll. The secretaries got a kick out of this. Also, since I was the youngest guy in the office, they went out of their way to help me produce quality products. I had learned a quick lesson the day I proudly presented my boss my first paper. I was so excited that I failed to proofread it properly. It had two typos. From that time forward I performed a line-buy-line proof read of everything, and quickly established a reputation for producing good papers. A lot of them ended up in the Congressional Record.

My boss, Colonel Partick N. Delavan had been an early commander of the UTT Helicopter Company, and since I had served in that unit on my first tour, he took me under his wing. We would work together late at night to answer questions from the Congress about our programs. Any paper going to them had to have signatures on it from several staff agencies in the Pentagon. These signatures were called 'chops,' and signified that each agency had seen the paper and was in agreement with it. For example, any paper that had a number in it had to be 'chopped' by the Comptroller of The Army. He was responsible for keeping track of all numbers we gave to Congress, hopefully to prevent errors.

Colonel Delavan didn't have much use for this bureaucratic nonsense. It caused a lot of pressure because we only had a few hours to write and coordinate these papers and get them over to the 'Hill' (as we called the U.S. Congressional buildings). To expedite them late at night, Colonel Delavan taught me how to take a signature off of an old paper and use the copying machine to place it on a new one. We moved a lot of papers, and to my knowledge, no harm was done.

During this assignment I remained on flying status. The Army had a fleet of T-42 twin engine transport aircraft at Fort Belvour, Virginia to support the Army Staff. I was able to get one of them anytime I wanted it. I was required to meet several minimum requirements to continue to be eligible for flight pay. The basic requirement was that I had to fly at least four hours a month. Most of the time I found it difficult to get time off from my desk job to fly. For safety reasons I always flew with another person, rotating pilot and copilot duties.

The T-42 was a fast little four seat aircraft with retractable landing gear. It flew at about two hundred and eighty mph and we could easily fly one thousand miles on a tank of fuel. We got around the country with ease. Occasionally we would fly up to Maine and buy live lobsters. On one trip we were coming back home at night and the lobsters, which were in the back seat, got out of their cage and started crawling around. The first I knew about it was when I felt something crawling on my shoulder. What an eerie feeling! I was flying and when I jumped it sent the aircraft into a dive. My copilot, not knowing what was going on, grabbed the controls. I finally convinced him to pull out a flashlight and have a look. Laughing, he managed to get the critters back in their container. Needless to say, it took a while to get our adrenaline back to normal levels.

On another trip I had called Mary Jane's parents and arranged for them to meet me at an airport near their Tennessee home. Her father raised pigs and had been looking for a way to get some fresh pork to his grandchildren. He agreed to deliver a box of fresh meat to the aircraft. We landed near Cookeville, and he loaded a huge Styrofoam cooler full of about one hundred pounds of pork. It completely filled the back seat. On the flight home my copilot could not help but ponder what would happen if we crashed and burned. We laughed about the prospect of some poor recovery team trying to identify the body of the back seat passenger. Such is the grim humor of pilots.

On a trip back from St Louis one night I had my only brush with aviation disaster during this tour. I was flying at ten thousand feet in clear air over a cloud deck. About one hundred miles from Washington, D.C., I received radio clearance from air traffic control to descend down through the clouds. I let down into the clouds and immediately found that the aircraft was picking up heavy ice. I had turned on the anti-ice devices, but they could not keep up with the rapid build-up. I called air traffic control and was cleared to climb but when I added power, I could not stop my descent. With the throttles fully open I was still descending at about two hundred feet per minute. I knew that between me and my destination and in all directions around me stood a range of mountains. The way the descent was going it was only a matter of time until I flew into the ground.

I was at the point of panic when I suddenly broke out of the clouds. Simultaneously, I cleared the mountain range by about one thousand feet and saw before me the bright lights of the entire Washington D.C. area. What a beautiful sight! The warmer air quickly melted the ice. It made a terrible rattling noise as it flew off in chunks and bounced off of the tail of the aircraft. Within fifteen minutes I had landed safely and was once again counting my blessings and wondering why I wanted to be a pilot in the first place.

Shortly after this close call I was offered a great career opportunity. I was nominated by my branch to be the Army Aide de Camp to the Chairman of the Joint Chiefs of Staff. At that time the Chairman, who is the senior military man in uniform, was a U.S. Air Force General named Jones. I was excited about the job because during the interview process, I was told that if selected, I would be checked out in the Air Force jet aircraft that the Chairman flew, and would fly as his copilot. I went through several interviews and the competition got down to two officers. After a final interview the other officer was selected. I was told that he was picked because he was not married, and that the Chairman traveled a lot and did not want to take me away from my family after three tours in Vietnam. As it turned out, it is a good thing I didn't get the job because I got a better one a few months later.

In late 1974 the Secretary of the Army embarked on a tour of the different Army bases, and occasionally invited an Army Staff Officer to accompany him. I was selected to accompany him on a visit to the Army Aviation Center at Fort Rucker, where I had attended flight training. We flew down on his four engine executive jet. It was white with 'United States of America' written in blue on the side. Other than the flight crew there was only three of us on the aircraft. We got a VIP welcome by the Commander, Major General Maddux, who had been my boss when I originally reported to the Pentagon. He welcomed me by name and I really felt important.

I stayed in the same guesthouse with the Secretary, ate my meals with him and we attended a reception at General Maddux's home that evening. During briefings and tours the next day the Secretary would ask me questions and I made notes. We flew back to Washington that night. Later, I wrote an after action report which was widely read around the Pentagon. I was getting a taste of power and felt sure I was being groomed for something important.

In my second year in the Pentagon I was given an assignment that involved giving individual briefings to several General Officers. One of the Generals I briefed had a reputation for being tough on Action Officers. I spent a couple of hours alone with him and answered at least a hundred questions. Finally, he was satisfied and later told my boss that I had done a good job. I soon learned that I had gotten 'face time' with the General. In doing so I had given him a chance to get to know me, which would soon influence an important decision.

About 6 months later I was surprised to find my name on the promotion list to Lieutenant Colonel. I was not in the zone of consideration, and had again been selected for early promotion. As it turned out, the General that I had briefed had served as the President of the Promotion Board. In the Army you never know who or what will make a difference in your career.

Shortly after getting on the promotion list, I was selected for command of an aviation battalion. That was the very first year the Army had conducted centralized selection of battalion commanders. Up until that time they had been picked by the local senior commander, who was often influenced by politics. In order to insure that the best and brightest got selected, the Army started conducting selection boards just like promotion boards. These boards not only selected the commanders, they designated where each officer would command.

Prior to the command board meeting I had been required to submit a preference sheet stating my first three choices for my next assignment. I had listed Hawaii as my first choice. A few weeks after the board results were released I was informed by telephone that I was going to get my first choice: the Aviation Battalion of the 25th Infantry Division in Hawaii. I called Mary Jane to tell her the good news. I said that I was going to slowly spell the location and for her to let me know when she figured it out. I only got through two letters, H-A-... when she screamed in delight. It was a dream that had come true for both of us.

My boss at the time, Colonel Earl W. Sharp, tried to throw a monkey wrench in my departure. He objected because I would be leaving after only two years on the Army Staff. The normal tour was three years, and up until that time was almost never changed. I was really concerned because if I stayed another year I would miss the command in Hawaii, and no telling where I would end up. I argued strongly to be released and the decision was finally made in the front office by the three stars Director of Operations. He said the Army Staff had to support the new centralized command selection process if it was to succeed. Finally, I got orders and we prepared to depart. A few days later I was promoted, given a Meritorious Service Medal, and sent on my way to Hawaii.

We arrived at the airport in Hawaii and were met by the outgoing commander and his wife, Dick and Katie Antross. In about thirty minutes we found ourselves at the Royal Hawaiian Hotel in Waikiki. This was to be our temporary home while I processed into the Division. As a battalion commander, I was given priority for housing and got the next one available, which took about a week. Our stay in the hotel, which was the oldest and most famous one there, convinced the family that we were in for a great tour. It turned out even better than we thought possible.

The 25th Division was located at Schofield Barracks, which is in the center of the island of Oahu. It is located about twenty miles up the hill from Honolulu and Pearl Harbor. Since Oahu is relatively small, the Division's primary training area is about one hundred miles away on the island of Hawaii, also known as the Big Island. This training area, named Pahakaloa, was located between two huge volcanoes and at about four thousand feet above sea level. It presented a hostile training environment with lots of wind and volcanic dust. The high altitude and low air density was especially tough on helicopters, and required special training for pilots before they could fly there. This training area was to become the source of most of my problems during the next three years.

I had arrived in Hawaii a few weeks before I was due to assume command, so was assigned a temporary job that I really didn't want.

The Commander of the Division's Air Cavalry Squadron had been accused of some wrong doings, and I was directed to conduct an investigation and recommend action, if appropriate. Other than the aviation battalion that I was going to command, the cavalry squadron was the only other large unit with helicopters. Also, as the aviation battalion commander I would have an additional duty as the Division Aviation Staff Officer, where I would over-watch all aviation related activities in the Division. I really didn't want to get involved in investigating a member of the aviation community, but had no choice. As it turned out, the officer was found guilty and taken out of command. Fortunately, this outcome did not significantly influence my relationships the new cavalry squadron commander as I had feared.

On 1 July 1975 I assumed command of a battalion with over seven hundred people and one hundred aircraft. It was probably the largest aviation battalion in the Army, and about the same size as the brigade I was to command a few years later. I was also probably the youngest aviation battalion commander at that time. The executive officer was older than I was and several of the company commanders were the same age. This, however, made no difference. My extensive combat experience and Army staff assignment gave me instant credibility with both the members of my unit and my bosses.

The battalion was so large because in addition to the normal aviation units found in an Infantry Division, I had assigned an additional assault helicopter company and a medium lift helicopter company. The additional companies were units that had been moved to Hawaii from Vietnam. One was the 118th Assault Helicopter Company that had Hueys and Cobras, and the other was the 147th Assault Support Helicopter Company that was equipped with Chinooks. The 147th had been the mother company for the Chinook Platoon that had been part of my command in Vietnam. They had the same pocket patch and the same radio call sign, 'Hill Climber.'

My first challenge had nothing to do with aircraft. The Sergeant Major told me that there was considerable unrest among the young enlisted men in the unit. Most of them were holdovers from the draft that was about to be phased out. I established an open door policy that allowed any soldier to walk into my office unannounced and voice complaints. I also started a monthly closed-door session with an 'enlisted council,' which consisted of one representative from each platoon sized unit in the battalion, about 30 men. There were no other people allowed into the room.

The first complaint I heard was that the First Sergeants of the companies were taking the light bulbs out of the stairwells at night to save on electrical expenses. The Army had a tight budget at the time. Electric meters had been installed in each unit area. First Sergeants were been judged on their ability to operate with a low electric bill.

I ordered all electric bulbs replaced and lights turned on that night. The men had instant feedback that their suggestions were taken seriously. The word got out and the complaints slowly dried up as problems were solved. However, I don't think the Non-Commissioned Officers ever forgave me for what they saw as going behind their backs.

I had gone into the assignment with my number one priority being aviation safety. I had already seen too much death, and was determined not lose a man during the entire command tour. By putting safety before mission accomplishment, I was able to succeed. However, this often caused friction with the units I was supporting because their commanders expected the 'do or die' aviation support they had received in Vietnam.

A lot of our flying was over water between the islands of the State. To prepare for a potential emergency landing in water we had to practice special flying techniques and carry special equipment. During the first month of command I underwent training for over-water flight, which involved jumping out of a helicopter into the ocean, inflating a life vest then a life raft, climbing into the raft, then being 'rescued' by a U.S. Coast Guard helicopter. The 'rescue' consisted of being pulled up about fifty feet on a winch to the helicopter.

When my turn came and I got up there I was expecting to be swung into the aircraft, but the winch operator just put a chocolate chip cookie in my mouth and lowered me back into the water. I was picked up later by my own helicopter. I did not know it at the time, but an Army photographer was on my helicopter and took a picture of me hanging from the Coast Guard aircraft. The picture and an article about the training appeared in the local Army newspaper, and then made it onto the front page of the Army Times, a worldwide weekly publication. My command tour was off to a good start.

At that time Army Aviation was going through a transition from Vietnam era flying to preparing for a war in Europe. The primary difference was the air defense threat. It was felt that in order to survive on the European battlefield, helicopters would have to operate exclusive at low level, or 'nap-of-the-earth' altitudes. Therefore, I was directed to develop a training course that would teach my aviators the correct techniques for this type flying. It was different because it consisted of hovering behind trees and hilltops, then flying rapidly to the next hiding place. With our single engine aircraft it was high-risk operations. Any significant maintenance problem would put an aircraft into the trees. Luckily, the battalion had no NOE related accidents while I was in command.

Maintenance problems turned out to have caused the first of three helicopter crashes the battalion was to suffer under my command. The first one was reported to me while I was setting in a barber's chair getting my hair trimmed. One of my officers popped in the door and said that a CH-47 Chinook had crashed. I jumped out of the chair and immediately assumed the worst. I could only think of the two Chinooks that I had lost in Vietnam. The potential for loss of life was enormous because CH-47s routinely carried up to thirty troops between training areas.

Upon arrival at my headquarters I began to get some facts. The crash had happened on the island of Hawaii at the Division's Pahakaloa training area. I was greatly relieved to find out that there were no serious injuries. Then I got the bad news. The aircraft had been a total loss. The CH-47 has two sets of rotor blades and when they rotate, they intermesh. One of the transmissions had failed and its blades had smashed into the other set, ripping the aircraft apart and setting it on fire. The aircraft had just landed and was on the ground when the accident occurred. The crew was able to scurry out of the debris with only cuts and bruises. Fortunately, there had been no passengers on board.

As is standard procedure following any peacetime Army aircraft accident, a team of investigators from the Army Safety Center showed up the next day to conduct an accident investigation. Their mission was to determine the cause of the accident and recommend corrective action that would prevent future accidents. They concluded the accident was caused by a bad transmission. My unit was absolved of all blame.

The fault was assigned to the factory that had built the transmission. If pilot or maintenance error had been determined to be the cause of the accident, big black marks would have been placed on the record of the unit and all commanders in the chain of command, including my bosses. Therefore, we were tremendously relieved when the accident report was published.

I was not so lucky when the second and third accidents occurred a few months later. They were related accidents that again took place on the Big Island, this time on top of one of the ten thousand feet volcanoes. At that altitude the air is so thin that a helicopter can barely fly. Most helicopters can not hover at that altitude. On this day a flight of two AH-1 Cobras that were flying from Pahakaloa back to Oahu decided to climb up to the top of one of the volcanoes and take some pictures. They ignored a prohibition on departing from their direct flight route home.

When they got to the top of the mountain they did not notice that the wind was blowing at about fifty mph. Thus, when flying into the wind at about sixty mph indicated airspeed, the aircraft was moving over the ground at only ten mph. The pilot of one of the aircraft took his eyes off of the airspeed indicator and turned down wind. He was using the ground as a reference and attempted to maintain the slow ground speed so the copilot could take pictures. With a fifty mph tail wind, the aircraft had to actually fly backwards at forty mph to maintain a ground speed of ten mph. Thus, as the aircraft slowed through zero mph indicated airspeed it simply stopped flying and fell to the ground. The crew was unhurt. They exited the crash and signaled the other aircraft that they were ok.

The wing aircraft reported the crash on the radio but wisely decided not to try to land. An OH-58 Kiowa that was flying nearby monitored the call for help and flew up the mountain to the crash site. Upon arrival, the pilot decided to try to land and help. As he slowed to a hover this aircraft also fell out of the air and crashed. Now we had two crews on the ground but fortunately, nobody was seriously injured. Finally, a CH-47 responded to the call for help. It was the only type of aircraft in the battalion that had the power to land at ten thousand feet, so was able to get in to rescue the crews and later, haul out what was left of the crashed aircraft.

As before, these accidents were investigated. This time pilot error was determined to be the cause. These two accidents became known at our higher headquarters as the 'Hawaii Double Header,' and gained the Division some attention it did not need. The higher headquarters, known as Forces Command, decided to send an inspection team to inspect all aspects of our aviation operations and training program. They found some problems that we were required to correct. This caused me considerable worry and concern for a couple of months. After a re-check about ninety days later, they gave us a clean bill of health, and the pressure was off. I decided that I did not care much for peacetime aviation procedures.

Toward the end of my command tour the Army decided to put women into aviation units. None of us in the battalion had any experience in dealing with female soldiers, so we had to learn the hard way. I basically turned the whole thing over to my Command Sergeant Major Robert Bratton. When the women showed up he initially tried to treat them differently from the men.

He assigned them separate living quarters in the barracks and separate tents and bathroom facilities in the field. While conducting field training he would truck them back to the barracks every day for showers. However, all of this special treatment slowly faded away as he found out that the women did not want special treatment. They continued to have separate facilities in the barracks but in the field, they were integrated with the men as much as possible. Maintaining privacy became their problem. The women did their jobs and the major problem that I had feared never developed.

During the mid-1970s the Department of the Army designated the length of battalion command tours at eighteen months. A few years later they moved it to two years. I was stuck with having to give up command at the eighteen month point of my three year tour in Hawaii. The Commanding General selected me to serve as his Inspector General. In this job I was provided with a staff of about twenty people with which to conduct recurring inspections of all units within the Division. Specifically, I was charged with insuring that all Army standards and procedures were being implemented and properly used. I reported the results of the inspections, both the good and the bad, directly to the General. Therefore, I was a key player in determining the success or failure of every commander in the Division.

At the time I took this job the inspection system in place was hated in the Division. It was an unannounced inspection at company level, and each company would get one inspection each year. My office would secretly schedule the inspections and inform only the Division Chief of Staff what unit was next. At 6:00 AM on the morning of an inspection one of my assistants would call the selected company and direct them to cancel all planned activities for the day and prepare for the inspection. My team would show up at 8:00 AM and begin a detailed examination of ever aspect of the unit. Nothing was off limits. By mid-afternoon I would get reports from all of my inspectors, look over the results, and decide if the unit passed or failed. At 4:00 PM I would give the unit a briefing on results.

How well the unit did usually had a big impact on how well the unit's commanders did on their efficiency reports, and a failure could result in relief from command (being fired). I took no pleasure in telling a bright eyed young commander that his unit had failed. This assignment taught me how to deal with giving people bad news. Up until that time, dealing with bad news had been a weak point in my career.

The Inspector General job was one of the least favorite of all that I attempted in my career. Some of the battalion and brigade commanders who had been good friends when I was in command avoided me while others tried to butter me up. I mostly tried to stay away from them and just get my job done. After about a year in the job I was notified that I had been selected to attend the U.S. Army War College at Carlisle Barracks, Pennsylvania. This was what every officer who commanded a battalion wanted. Only a small percentage of officers were selected to attend this school, which is a one year course and is the highest level school in the Army. It is literally designed to prepare the best and brightest for promotion the General Officer.

During the final months of my tour in Hawaii I found time to focus on my family. The Army had a recreation area near the small town of Waianae, on the west side of Oahu. It had small wooden cabins with primitive accommodations. They fronted directly on a beautiful white sand beach. I could get a cabin any time I wanted, and they only cost a few Dollars per night. We would load up the station wagon with food and all kinds of swimming and beach gear and spend wonderful weekends there.

Bill was old enough take scuba diving lessons. I bought dive equipment for both of us and we took lessons to qualify for ocean diving. We went for several dives off of the beach at Waianae, and brought back lots of coral and sea-shells. This went on until Bill somehow got separated from me on the bottom during one dive. I searched everywhere for him with no luck. Finally, after I had given him up for dead and got back in the boat, he surfaced about one hundred yards away. It was a stressful few minutes for me. I was already trying to figure out how to give his mother the bad news. Shortly after that dive we sold all of our dive gear. Bill bought a bicycle and I bought a stereo.

Sometime during the tour we made up our minds that we would someday return to Hawaii. We started looking around for some property in which to invest. We found an acre lot with a small house on it. It was on the north shore on top of a hill looking west over the ocean. We fell in love with it and bought it. With those roots planted and a determination to return someday, we reluctantly departed the Islands for Pennsylvania.

CHAPTER 15

WRAPPING IT UP

Upon arrival at Carlisle Barracks in June 1978, we were assigned a small house on post. All around us were families with lots of children. Our children loved it, especially all of the snow in the winter. I worked hard in the course, which consisted mostly of lectures and seminars on national and international level subject such as budgets and organizations. There were no exams or grades in the course, which made it even more enjoyable. The best part was getting to slow down and meet some of my contemporaries. About twenty percent of my classmates would eventually be promoted to General Officer. Fortunately or unfortunately (don't know which), I was not to be one of them.

Toward the end of the course in May 1979, I got a telephone call from a friend that worked in the Pentagon. He told me that he had seen the yet unpublished Colonels promotion list and that my name was on it. This was another great surprise because I was not in the primary promotion zone. This was my third early promotion. I had been selected for promotion with eighteen years of service, three years earlier than most officers.

I entered a period of intense negotiations with the Field Artillery Branch regarding my follow-on assignment. They wanted to send me back to the Pentagon as a staff officer. I badly wanted to stay on the command track, and my family did not want to go back to Washington, so I started looking around for alternatives. There were only four Colonel-level aviation commands in the Army at that time and I wanted one of them. The most desirable one was the 6th Cavalry Brigade at Fort Hood, Texas. I decided that if I could position myself at Fort Hood, I would have a better shot at getting that command.

A couple of things happened at about the same time that resulted in me getting what I wanted. First, I made my wishes known to my assignments officer. About the same time the current Brigade Commander, Colonel (later Major General) Bob Molinelli, was diagnosed with cancer. A decision was made to assign me as his Deputy Commander to help run the unit while he went through chemotherapy. With orders in hand I made a trip to Fort Hood and bought a house. We reported for duty there in July 1979.

Soon after my arrival Colonel Molinelli burst my bubble. He told me that I need not expect to command the brigade because I was an Artillery Officer. He was an Armor Officer and there was great competition between the branches for command slots. Sure enough, when the command board met that year, another officer was selected to replace Bob.

In about a year I was promoted to Colonel and reassigned to the 3d Corps Staff as an Assistant Operations Officer. I stayed there for two years. I bought a sailboat, rebuilt a Ford Mustang convertible and generally had a good time with the family. But as an aviator in an armor assignment, I was a fish out of water. I did not like my job or my bosses, and I failed to be selected for command both of those years. I concluded that the Army had forgotten about me.

One bright spot during the tour was my son Bill's appointment to the U.S. Military Academy. During his junior year in high school he started to express interest in the military. He was making good grades so I decided to start the paperwork for a nomination to West Point. We submitted the application to Congressman Al Gore, who nominated him. Gore's nomination put Bill in competition with nine other people for the appointment.

After an extensive evaluation and grading period, Bill was selected and presented with the appointment. He was only seventeen years old. With some apprehension we put him on an airplane bound through New York to West Point. Needless to say, we anxiously sat by the telephone that night until he called to report his safe arrival.

As I neared the end of my three year tour at Fort Hood, Mary Jane and I decided we wanted to go back to Hawaii. My branch assignment officer at that time was a friend from the old UTT. He arranged a job as a Joint Staff Officer at the U.S. Pacific Command at Camp Smith, Hawaii. I happily accepted this assignment, concluding that my career was at a dead end, and that we would be able to fulfill our dream of retiring in Hawaii. We sold our house in Texas, bought one in Hawaii, and moved the family there in May 1982. Nonna was the only one in the family that was unhappy with the move. She was to be a senior in high school and wanted to stay in Texas to graduate.

About a year after we arrived back in Hawaii, and two weeks before she was to graduate from high school, Nonna unexpectedly and tragically died from a case of bacterial meningitis. This was such a shock to us all! We had been living the American dream and now it was shattered. It changed our outlook and fondness for Hawaii, and caused me to start looking around for some way to send our life in a different direction. I found it when I was finally selected for brigade command. By this time the Army had decided to place an aviation brigade in all of its divisions, and I was selected to organize and command the very first of these in the 7th Infantry Division at Fort Ord, California.

The 7th was going to be reorganized into a 'light infantry' division. This was the brainchild of the Army Chief of Staff who wanted to reduce the size and equipment of all 'foot' infantry divisions. The plan was to almost eliminate trucks and heavy equipment so that the 'light fighters' could be rapidly transported anywhere in the world in only a few days. It sounded like a great concept and I was excited to be selected to be part of it.

We reluctantly placed both of our Hawaii properties on the market and departed for California. It was hard to make this drastic change of direction but we reduced the pain by anticipating the new job and life on the beautiful Monterey Peninsula. We arrived at the regional airport on a small commuter airplane. It was about 10:00 PM at night and there was a thin fog over Monterey and Fort Ord, which made the approach and landing a sensational visual experience. We were met at the airport by Lieutenant Colonel Jim Davidson and his family. Jim was designated to become my Executive Officer. The greetings were warm and we were off to a great start.

Unfortunately, things turned sour immediately. In order to keep the following paragraphs about my tour at Fort Ord from sounding like sour grapes, I will not use any names.

Remembering the great reception I received at Schofield Barracks when I reported for battalion command duty, I was expecting to be welcomed into the 7th Infantry Division family with some enthusiasm and warmth. Instead, the Division Commander at that time and his staff treated me as an uninvited guest. To make matters worse, The Post Commander, a Colonel consumed in his own self-importance, refused to designate a set of family quarters for us. He had several empty houses but was 'saving' them for some of his own staff.

After about two weeks of my family living in a motel room, I made a big fuss and threatened to complain to the Commanding General. The Post Commander grudgingly assigned me a small house in an area of lower ranking officers. All of the other brigade commanders lived together in a cluster of newer houses. My feeling of isolation increased. I was to find out later that there was a strong bias throughout the Division against Army Aviation and Army Aviators. This was to cloud my entire stay at Fort Ord. Amplified by a new Division Commander who assumed command a few months later, this bias would ultimately end any chance I had for further promotion.

I did not have a brigade when I arrived at Fort Ord. My first challenge was to develop a plan to reorganize the various aviation assets in the Division from separate units into a new brigade structure. At the time of my arrival the 7th Infantry Division had the lowest priority of all of the Divisions in the Army. This meant that the 7th got what was left after every other Division was issued their equipment and personnel. Our priority was increased as we started transition to the 'light' configuration. I received thirty two new UH-60 Blackhawk Helicopters but was stuck with the oldest AH-1 Cobras and OH-58 Kiowas in the active Army.

Compounding my problems was the introduction of several training requirement that were developed for the infantry units that had almost no equipment to maintain other than their individual and crew served weapons. Ignoring the fact that helicopter maintenance was a full time job, the Division Commander decreed that aviation units would be required to complete the same forced marches and physical training exercises as the Infantry. The end result was my mechanics routinely worked twelve hours per day and seven days a week. This had a predictable negative impact on morale and efficiency, and greatly complicated efforts to maintain our older aircraft.

There was tremendous pressure from above for accident free aviation operations. Shortly after his arrival, the new Commander took me aside and quietly told me that he did not trust aviators and that he would have my rear end when (my pilots) crashed one of his helicopters. This pressure was not needed because I gave aviation safety first priority over all other activities. This was a carryover from my earlier days when so many of my friends and subordinates had been needlessly killed in accidents.

I was absolutely bound by Army Regulations to accept and comply with the weather forecast provided by the U.S. Air Force Forecaster attached to my brigade. If he said that the weather was below minimums for flight operations, my units could not fly. This was never understood by some of the other brigade commanders in the Division. One example was an incident when the Division Artillery Commander called me and insisted that he could look up from his location in the field and see clear blue sky. He insisted that I overrule the weather forecaster and send him some aircraft.

There had been a joke around aviation for years about a non-aviator with such little understanding of flight operations the he would make that exact remark. I thought at first he was trying to be funny. When I tried to explain that the airfield was fogged in, and that I did not have the authority to overrule the forecaster, he became indignant and said he was going to report me to our boss. I never heard any more about it.

We had one brigade commander that was not a 'climber' (individual that climbs over the backs of others to advance himself). I had met Colonel Robert 'Bob' Ord III, in Vietnam when my unit provided helicopter support to his advisory team. At Fort Ord he routinely sought my advice and recommendations on air assault operations, and understood my peacetime flying limitations. He would later command his own Division and be promoted to Lieutenant General.

It was standard practice for the Infantry and Artillery units to spend several days cleaning and spit shining their equipment after returning from field training exercises. However, the aviation units did not have this luxury because of the enormous demand for aircraft maintenance that followed field training. That did not keep the Division Commander from holding us to the same standard as the ground units. On one occasion he drove unannounced to one of my units and asked to look inside their equipment containers.

The equipment had been hastily put away upon return from the field with the intent of thoroughly cleaning it after completing several critical aircraft maintenance tasks. The General went nuts. He screamed and yelled at everybody in sight and then came to my office and told me how sorry my unit was. He had absolutely no understanding of our need to prioritize activities. This was the only time in my career that a boss 'chewed me out.'

For two years my units flew mostly at night using night vision devices, and flying into and out of tight landing zones located in the mountains of California. Our flight operations were second only to Special Operations units in levels of difficulty and risk. In spite of all of the odds, there were no injury accidents in the brigade during my command tour. I suspect that there have been few aviation commanders to complete both battalion and brigade command without an injury accident. This is the career accomplishment of which I am most proud. It apparently meant little to my boss.

I have to admit that I failed to give him the adoration he demanded and received from the other brigade commanders. After he made it clear that he did not trust aviators, I knew that I would not receive his support for further advancement in the Army. Sure enough, when it came time for efficiency ratings, I was given the lowest rating of my career. He actually said, and I quote from the report: "Jerry is a low-key performer, almost bordering on reticence." In Army lingo this is known as 'the kiss of death' to a career. A few months later when the promotion list came out my name was not there. Almost all of my fellow brigade commanders were eventually promoted.

Along toward the end of my tour I started looking around for a follow-on job. I asked the Commander for some help but was given none. Suddenly late one night I received a phone call at home from Major General Pat Patrick. He was the Commanding General of the 101st Airborne Division (Air Assault) at Fort Campbell, Kentucky. He asked me if I would come to Fort Campbell and take over as his Chief of Staff. I accepted on the spot. This was one of the most sought after Colonel's jobs in the Army, and I couldn't believe I was going to get it.

I later found out that the key individual that influenced General Patrick's decision to hire me was Colonel Ben Couch, who was serving as the Aviation Brigade Commander in the 101st. Ben had been one of my company commanders, and later the Executive Officer of the 25th Aviation Battalion when I commanded it. Also, I must give credit to Mary Jane. Over the years she had built a great reputation for being a supportive Army wife.

My replacement was already on station so I quickly arranged a change of command ceremony and headed east. I departed with no sadness but recognized that what should have been the highlight tour of my career had been the low point, not because of my job but because of the lack of acceptance and support by my bosses.

Upon arrival at Fort Campbell I felt that I had finally returned to the real Army. My reception was enthusiastic and genuine. I had departed the poorest command environment in my career to arrive at the best. My family's house was waiting. My transition into the job was smooth. The best part was that General Patrick immediately gave me control over coordinating the activities of the twenty thousand soldiers of the Division and Fort Campbell.

I very quickly found out why the 101st was such an outstanding organization. Simply stated, it had first choice for people and equipment. It was politically well connected at Department of the Army level and was able to hand pick its commanders and senior NCOs. In addition, the 101st had priority over the rest of the Army for aircraft and aviation repair parts. At Fort Ord I had never been able to hand pick a single subordinate, and although we were told we had a high priority, I was never able to get enough repair parts to keep my aircraft availability rates much above the Army standard (about 75%). Now I knew where the new aircraft, best people and repair parts had gone.

A modern Army Division and the post on which it is located operates at the speed with which paperwork flows through the headquarters. This is because in the Army, nothing gets done without a piece of paper. I decided early that I would focus on moving the paper and getting the decisions made quickly. I wanted to be the 'inside man.' I left the 'outside work' such as visiting training events and inspecting operations to the two Assistant Division Commanders and the Post Commander.

My objective was to start every day with a clean 'in box.' To do this I often worked late into the night. I would start each day with a one hour private session with the Commanding General during which I briefed him and provided a recommendation on every item that required his signature or other action. He would then have the remainder of the day to get out of the office and interface with the troops, which is what I think a Division Commander should do with his time. General Patrick apparently appreciated the way I did my job. He gave me a top rating and worked very hard to get me promoted. I was again disappointed.

At this point, about one year into my job, General Patrick got his third star and moved to a new assignment is Korea. Major General Teddy Allen replaced him. General Allen had been free to exercise one of the unwritten rules in the Army, which is that a Division Commander has absolute freedom to pick any qualified officer he wants as his Chief of Staff. Fortunately, he elected to keep me in the job. His leadership style was very much like that of General Patrick so there was a smooth transition for everyone involved.

The one project that somewhat dominated my entire two years at Fort Campbell was closing-out all of the problems that had been generated when the Division suffered the loss of two hundred and forty eight soldiers who were on their way back from a peacekeeping mission in the Middle East. The accident had occurred on 12 December 1985 when their DC-8 crashed at Gander, Newfoundland.

General Patrick had gained nationwide attention for his compassionate handling of the disaster. When I assumed the Chief of Staff's job there were dozens of surviving wives and families still living near Fort Campbell. General Patrick had encouraged them to call on him and his staff to assist with any problems they might experience. There were all kinds of legal and insurance issues involved. I quickly learned that taking care of the Gander families was General Patrick's first priority. Therefore, I spent a tremendous amount of time working with the staff to solve problems and keep the surviving wives and their families happy.

Upon assuming command, General Allen tried to get beyond Gander by refocusing the Division's priorities on training and operations. This caused lots of problems because the Gander families continued to demand attention and assets. They had a sympathetic press and lots of political connections so my job became even more difficult. The crowning moment came when General Allen ordered the closing of the 'Widow Support Center,' a building that General Patrick had made available for the widows to gather, hold meetings and makes free long distance telephone calls. This building was located near the main gate to the Post and was a symbol of the Division's focus on the Gander aftermath. The closing caused an outcry from the widows and the community that echoed into the national press.

The issue finally subsided after we dedicated a memorial park in memory of the fallen soldiers. It contained a tree for each soldier and now is a centerpiece at Fort Campbell as a beautiful and fitting tribute to those soldiers and their families. The lessons I learned working with the Gander families came in handy near the end of my tour when the Division suffered another major aviation accident.

At about 11:00 PM one night I got a call from the Commander of the Division's Aviation Brigade. He reported that two of his Blackhawk helicopters had collided in flight while on a night training mission killing about twenty. He had no further details. Even without any facts, I knew this was going to be a major event for the Division and Fort Campbell.

I usually tried to stay in the background and let my staff do their job, but on this one I knew there would be no room for error. Therefore, I tracked every activity and personally planned and supervised the huge memorial service that was conducted a few days later. As tough as it was, we somehow got through this period and went back to work

About half way through my tour at Fort Campbell I was offered the honor of going back to Tennessee Tech University, my former College at Cookeville, Tennessee to be the guest of honor at their annual Commissioning Ceremony for their graduating ROTC cadets. Early on the morning of 6 June 1987 I departed Fort Campbell at the controls of a UH-1 Huey. I took great delight in landing the helicopter on the front lawn of the University President.

In 1988 I had one more shot at getting promoted. I knew that one Aviation Branch Colonel was usually selected each year, and I hoped it would be me. I thought I had a good shot because the 18th Airborne Corps Commander, Lieutenant General John Foss, had asked me if I wanted to stay at Fort Campbell as an Assistant Division Commander when I got promoted. Instead, I was notified by General Allen that I was again not selected. The board had picked another aviator who was serving as the Chief of Staff of another Division. This officer had the good fortune to have his Division Commander on the selection board, which usually made a difference.

The hard-to-take part of this was that the new aviation Brigadier General was assigned to the 101st as an Assistant Division Commander, the job that LTG Foss had earlier asked me if I wanted. I was assigned the task of being his sponsor and helping him get oriented in the job. Needless to say, my heart was not in it, but I did the best I could under the circumstances.

By this time I had almost two years in the Chief of Staff's job and was tired of working twelve hours a day and being on call twenty four hours a day. Mary Jane and I made the hard decision that it was time to depart the 101st. I talked to my assignment officer and he wanted me to go back to the Pentagon to enhance my chances of promotion next year. I was simply fed up with the whole thing. I checked around and found out that the job of Deputy Chief of Staff for Operations and Plans (DCSOPS) at Western Command, Fort Shafter, Hawaii was coming open. Here was a chance to get back to Hawaii and get established before our planned retirement there. I went after the job and got it. We were given a series of impressive and emotional farewell ceremonies and departed to begin our last assignment.

I spent the final two years of my military career supervising a staff of about one hundred people. I was responsible for managing the Operations and Training Budget of about one hundred million Dollars per year. Our command was directly subordinate to Department of the Army, so I frequently traveled to Washington, D.C. for meetings and briefings in the Pentagon. The Cold War had ended and the most dangerous threat to world peace at that time was considered to be the Iraqi Army.

About one and one half years into the assignment I realized that I was approaching ten years in grade as a Full Colonel. I decided that was enough. I retired at a small ceremony at Fort Shafter on 1 August 1990. Had I known that America would go to war with Iraq in less than a year, I might have stayed to participate in one more fight. Fifteen years later I still miss the Army. I often dream about my service. Most often my dreams go to the wonderful people with whom I worked and lived. I have finally concluded that people and relationships, especially family, are all that really matters in life.

Our Army in decisively engaged in both Iraq and Afghanistan as I write this. Army Aviation is playing a big role in these insurgencies. Therefore, a few months ago I prepared a short article outlining the Cardinal Rules that served me so well over forty years ago. I then published them on the Internet with the hope that the Rules would somehow make their way to today's Army aviators. They should find them useful in developing their own Cardinal Rules for Attack Helicopter Combat for the 21st Century.

Mary Jane and our youngest son Thomas join me for my final military formation. Bill, who had graduated from West Point, was on active duty and unable to attend.

Shortly before my retirement I had the honor of being on active duty with both of my sons. William, right, completed 20 years and retired in 2004. Thomas plans to complete his career and retire in about 2010.

CPSIA information can be obtained at www.ICGtesting.com
Printed in the USA
LVOW06s2143020913

350694LV00003B/243/A

9 781420 882582

Made in the USA
Middletown, DE
01 December 2022

16669664R00018

There's also the story of the bees. When the hive was destroyed, I was just as upset as when Meredith's mother inflicted yet another atrocity on her children.

Grandpa is the perfect counterpoint to this: he's always there for Meredith, and he always knows what to say and do.

On all of those levels, as well as others, this is a satisfying novel. It's one-of-a-kind, to begin with. It's a refreshing diversion from the current saturation of iffy narration of irrelevant family affairs.

Meredith is encouraged to become his shadow, assisting with them and learning about them. And she learns about life as he educates her about the hive's community, the various bees and their responsibilities, and their dances.

This novel has a lot of facets to it. Of course, there's Meredith's narrative, as well as her mother's, which is hinted at throughout the film as we wonder why she's so damaged - a subject that grows more pressing as Meredith returns to see her blameless father.

able to enjoy and be inspired by him. That's incredible, in my opinion.... In this book, he'll live on."

Meredith's story begins when she is five years old. Her mother uproots her and her younger brother from the family home and relocates them to their grandparents' house across the country. There is no explanation. Then Mom falls into a deep despair, withdraws to her room, and leaves the children in the care of their grandparents. Grandpa, a delightfully kind and intelligent guy, raises bees, and seeding — planting wildflowers in between crop rows, on motorway medians, on roofs, everywhere, not just in neighborhood gardens — would be the simplest and most useful thing we could do."

She says that it's what her grandfather, to whom "The Honey Bus" is dedicated, would want. "This is the part of the book that makes me the happiest: it made Grandpa immortal," May adds. "He was such a nice guy; you don't come across people like that anymore." Perhaps others will be

Daly City home she lives with her wife Jenn Jackson, a San Francisco Police Department lieutenant, until a few weeks ago. (Edith, the couple's 7-month-old golden retriever, was stung, prompting the move.)

May is frequently asked how people might aid the decreasing bee population during her ongoing book tour. "Bees need more fodder because we've paved over everything or erected monocultures, so they don't have a variety of blooms," she explains. "Guerrilla

"The Honey Bus" was acquired just a few weeks this time. It will be printed in 11 languages and distributed in 13 countries. It was just designated one of five must-read books by USA Today, and Bustle included it in a roundup of the finest new memoirs for spring.

May keeps six hives at San Francisco's Connecticut Friendship Garden in addition to writing (she has a female athlete in mind for a biography and is also planning a children's book). One of those hives was set up in the backyard of the

"It made her understand the flaw in her "The Honey Bus" manuscript: it was really a "monster-mom memoir," as she puts it. "It was in desperate need of a higher calling." My story is mainly about my grandfather and the bees rescuing me in an odd and amazing way. I completely reworked my proposal and memoir. 'It's a completely different book,' she commented after I called and sent it to her. We can go out with it once again.'

The rewriting took May seven months, but it was well worth it:

the experiences I had, I really freak out if I do something like that."

Despite the fact that May's proposal for "The Honey Bus" was rejected four years ago, one of the editors who saw it approached her to write "I, Who Did Not Die." The book, which was published in 2017, tells the story of Zahed Haftlang and Najah Aboud, two POWs on opposing sides of the Iran-Iraq War. "It really puts your own victimhood in harsh perspective," May says about the endeavor.

May left The Chronicle in the same year. Heather Karpas of ICM Partners, her book agent, circulated the proposal for "The Honey Bus." "I had a few nibbles, no bites," May adds, adding that she got despondent and spent time wallowing in bed, similar to her mother. May's funk, on the other hand, lasted barely a day or two, as opposed to her mother's years.

May confesses, "I was so scared I was going to turn into her." "In looking back, it was probably normal." But, because of

SECTION 4

“The Honey Bus” began as a graduate school thesis project for May. She authored a deluge of short tales while enrolled in an MFA program at Maryland's Goucher College in 2010 and 2011, half of which are included in "The Honey Bus" in some way. Peace didn't finish the book — or at least an early version of it — until she died in 2015.

tanks, while his hives were housed at other Big Sur locations.

and the honey-making process to a young May. "In the book, there are three voices: the young me, the adult me thinking on what happened, and the beekeeper/teacher me," she explains.

Her grandfather transformed a 1951 military bus into a honey manufacturing facility and named it the titular vehicle. The bus lay immobile on the family's land for decades, the seats and engine long since removed in favor of a spinner, pipes, rubber hoses, and storage teachings from her pleasant grandfather. May adds, "He spoke in metaphors, using the bees as models of correct behavior." "What he found honorable and admirable about bees' way of life became his moral ethic for humanity."

Bees, for example, live for the greater good, with each of their roles — from drone and field bees to nursing and queen bees — contributing to the "collective strength," as May describes it.

The reader is also educated as Grandpa describes bee behavior immediately assumed caregiving responsibilities for the siblings.

E. Franklin Peace, a plumber and beekeeper who May referred to as Grandpa, was Granny's second husband and May's step-grandfather. May explains, "I'm not blood connected to my grandpa, but I consider myself raised by him and reared by honeybees, which is funny, strange, and wonderful all at the same time."

May's memories of an absent mother and a devoted but frigid grandmother are mixed with life

10-year-old boy's rehabilitation from a terrible explosion in Iraq.

May, 49, is now sharing her own moving narrative, which she has been working on for approximately seven years.

She tells a fascinating story about life after her parents divorced when she was just shy of five years old in the book. May's mother moved from Rhode Island to California's Carmel Valley with her younger brother Matthew in tow. As their mother's melancholy worsened, they moved in with May's grandparents, who and being happy and astonished by what you discover."

May is the fifth generation of her family to maintain bees. She also worked at The Chronicle for 16 years as a reporter and feature writer, where she spent her days sharing other people's experiences. She was nominated for a Pulitzer Prize and received multiple prizes, including the PEN USA Literary Award for Journalism and the Casey Medal for Meritorious Journalism, for her "Operation Lion Heart" series, which chronicled a

SECTION 3

She took sanctuary in the wonderful world of these industrious pollinators as a child living up in a tumultuous environment, becoming lost in their buzzing virtuosity. She describes apiculture as "very contemplative" as an adult. "For me, the youthful amazement remains. It transports me back to that state of mind where everything is turned off and you're completely focused on what you're doing —

greater good. Meredith May's literary artistry is as sweet as nectar.

This book is necessary reading because it provides us with all we need to enter the bee's state of grace, just as honeybees do with their giving. Bees always give more than they take. Spending time aboard The Honey Bus has instilled in me a drive to be more of what someone else could require at this moment; perhaps this is the genuine nectar of the gods.

collective power. Meredith learned everything she couldn't from her birth parents while she fed off the Way of the Bees. In a sense, she was being raised by the bees. The author learned about compassion and how to flourish by caring for others from them.

We find ourselves dancing with the bees as we follow Meredith through the gateway into honeybee civilization. You'll be enthralled by the poetry of being in the presence of sacred beings who exist for the not only discovered the fascinating world of honeybees as her grandfather's beekeeping apprentice, but she also discovered her forever family.

The warmth of family is essential for bees. A solitary bee is unlikely to survive the night on its own. A beehive is based on a single principle: the family. I was aware of the nagging desire for a family.

May's wise, calm grandfather utilized the language of bees to convey old ways of persevering via

SECTION 2

May's interest over the rusted old Army bus in her grandfather's back yard was like a bee lured to honey. Meredith had a strong longing for the dilapidated honey bus. She yearned for permission to enter that gateway, knowing that amazing things took place inside her grandfather's top-secret laboratory. May's pleasure knew no boundaries on the day she was finally declared old enough for membership in the honey bus's secret club. Meredith

The voyage began with a swarm of bee stings that would terrify most kids. The temporary discomfort of being stung by swarms of bees, contrary to popular belief, built up a type of immunity against the more serious sting of feeling alone in the world.

grandfather would be a key lifeline for Meredith May, a young child whose life had been turned upside down and inside out by parental strife. Meredith's story, The Honey Bus, is enthralling in its depiction of how honeybees transformed a troubled kid into something beautiful. Franklin Peace began to introduce Meredith to the delights of beekeeping after sensing a desire for connection, caring, and something to replace the gaping hole in his granddaughter's mind.

about self-discovery and the natural world in general. A fascinating and inspiring book about family, bees, and how "nature has specific ways to keep [children] safe, even when they are overwhelmed with sadness."

A fascinating and inspiring book about family, bees, and how "nature has specific ways to keep [children] safe, even when they are overwhelmed with sadness. Honey has traditionally been regarded as a life elixir. The amazing powers of honey, bees, and her beekeeper behavior, has given her a feeling of calm and perspective. “"The more I learned about the inner world of honeybees, the more sense I was able to make of the outside world of people," she writes. May also integrates fascinating facts about honeybee social lives and roles into the story, and she portrays the process of generating honey and the function of the beekeeper in the lives of bees with affection. While honeybees are her subject, they serve as a springboard for a story inspecting hives, learning about bees, and eventually assisting him in harvesting honey in an old bus he had rigged up just for this purpose. May portrays her gratitude for the caring, dependable man who taught her to stretch out beyond her dysfunctional nuclear family and make her way into the wider world, encouraging her to go to college and not letting herself be defined by her mother's flaws. Her appreciation of nature, particularly the unexpected nuances of bee

SECTION 1

When Meredith May was five years old, her parents split. Her unstable, emotionally distant mother moved her and her younger brother to her mother's and mother's second husband rural property in California's Carmel Valley, where they tended beehives. After her mother took to her room and refused to deal with the kids, the author spent most of her non-school hours with "Grandpa," driving around in his old truck

Contents

SUMMARY OF THE HONEY BUS

MEREDITH MAY

a memoir of loss, courage and a girl saved by bees.

By YARA MATHEWS